THE EUROPEANS

JUDITH

By the same author

Stage Plays

Stripwell
Claw
The Love of a Good Man
Fair Slaughter
That Good Between Us
The Hang of the Gaol
The Loud Boy's Life
Birth on a Hard Shoulder
Crimes in Hot Countries
No End of Blame
Victory
The Power of the Dog
A Passion in Six Days
Downchild
The Castle
Women Beware Women (with Thomas Middleton)
The Possibilities
The Last Supper
The Bite of the Night
Scenes from an Execution
Seven Lears
Golgo
The Europeans
Judith

Radio Plays

One Afternoon on the 63rd Level of the North Face of the Pyramid of Cheops the Great
Henry V in Two Parts
Herman with Millie and Mick
Scenes from an Execution
The Early Hours of a Reviled Man.

Poetry

Don't Exaggerate; Desire and Abuse
The Breath of the Crowd
Gary the Thief/Gary Upright
Lullabies for the Impatient
The Ascent of Monte Grappa

Film

The Blow
The Castle

Essays

Arguments for a Theatre

PLAYSCRIPT 118

THE EUROPEANS
Struggles to Love

JUDITH
A Parting from the Body

Howard Barker

JOHN CALDER · LONDON
RIVERRUN PRESS · NEW YORK

First published in Great Britain, 1990, by
John Calder (Publishers) Ltd
9–15 Neal Street, London WC2H 9TU

and in the United States of America, 1990, by
Riverrun Press Inc
1170 Broadway, New York, NY 10001

British Library Cataloguing in Publication Data
Barker, Howard, 1946 -
The Europeans : struggles to love : Judith : parting from the body. - (Playscript; 118).
I. Title II. Series
822.914

IBSN 0-7145-4144-3

Library of Congress Cataloging in Publication Data
Barker, Howard.
The Europeans : struggles to love : Judith : parting from the body
Howard Barker.
p.198 cm.
Two plays.
ISBN 0-7145-4144-3 :
I. Title. II. Title: Judith.
PR6052. A6485E9 1990 90-35432
822' .914--dc20 CIP

Typeset in 9/10 pt Times by Pure Tech Corporation Pondicherry, India
Printed in Great Britain by Billing & Sons Ltd, Worcester

To
David Ian Rabey

THE EUROPEANS
Struggles to Love

CHARACTERS

LEOPOLD	Emperor of Austria
OFFICERS	Of the Imperial Army
TURKISH CAPTIVES	
THE PAINTER	Of the Imperial Court
STARHEMBERG	An Imperial General
THE EMPRESS	Of Austria
KATRIN	A Wounded Citizen
ORPHULS	A Priest
SUSANNAH	Sister of Katrin
IPSTEIN	An Imperial Minister
HARDENSTEIN	An Imperial Minister
FALLENGOTT	An Imperial Minister
GRUNDFELT	An Anatomist
BRUSTEIN	An Anatomist
PUPILS OF ANATOMY	
FIRST MOTHER	Parent of Orphuls
SECOND MOTHER	Parent of Starhemberg
FIRST BEGGAR	
SECOND BEGGAR	
THIRD BEGGAR	
FOURTH BEGGAR	
FIRST WOMAN BEGGAR	
SECOND WOMAN BEGGAR	
SERVANT	To the Empress
SHYBAL	A Common Soldier
McNOY	A Common Soldier
ARST	An Academician
FELIKS	An Academician
BOMBERG	An Academician
MIDWIFE	
LABOURERS	
JEMAL PASHA	A Turkish Commander

ACT ONE

Scene 1

A *plain, following a battle.*

LEOPOLD: **I laugh**
I laugh (*He walks towards some squatting* PRISONERS.)
I laugh
I laugh
Where's the painter? (*A* FIGURE *enters with an easel and board.*)
I laugh
I laugh (*The* PAINTER *sketches.*)
This pain which soddens every turf
This bowel which droops from every bush
This crop of widows and orphans
I laugh

OFFICER (*observing*): The Turks! The Turks!

LEOPOLD (*unmoved*): Fuck them. (*Some fire. The* OFFICERS *sheath their swords. The* PAINTER *paints.* LEOPOLD *kneels.*) Oh, God, I thank, Oh, God, I stoop, let all this Muslim flesh manure Christian ground, Oh, God, I bow, let all this scrag of Islam bring forth crops to feed the lowest labourer and he shall situate the crucifix above the lintel of the door and hang his weapon on its hook, and in the frosty fields his child shall kick the Tartar skull that ploughs dislodged —

OFFICERS (*unsheathing their weapons*): The Turks! The Turks!

LEOPOLD: Fuck them — (*Shellfire. The* PAINTER *rises anxiously.*) Are you afraid of dying?

PAINTER: No.

LEOPOLD: You don't mean no.

PAINTER: I do mean —

LEOPOLD: You say no, but you mean yes. You are afraid of dying, why?

PAINTER: I have this — I am under this — terrible illusion I am a decent painter and — as yet have little evidence — so —

LEOPOLD: **I laugh**
I laugh

PAINTER: Quite rightly but —

LEOPOLD: You think I am mad but the mad are the speakers of our time —
PAINTER: Yes —
LEOPOLD: Why?
PAINTER: Why —
LEOPOLD: Are they, yes?
PAINTER: I —
LEOPOLD: You say yes to everything I say, how will you ever be a decent painter?
PAINTER: I don't know —
LEOPOLD: Look at the prisoners, how they tremble like reeds on the lakeside as soon as their brothers come near, like a wind they come and go —

You lost
You lost

No fucking Seljuk lancers will cut you free, Ali! Draw them, record their bewilderment, they cannot understand why their god's quit, draw them!
OFFICER: The Turks! The Turks!
LEOPOLD: Oh, fuck your alarums, I am discussing art! (*Returning to his subject.*) This one in particular, who sports the topknot of his native land, squats with the distant look of one who senses execution in the offing, capture that. Though how you keep a pencil still in fingers that tremble as yours do, I can't imagine —
PAINTER: It's cold —
LEOPOLD: **It is cold, it is Europe!** (*A general hurrah breaks out among the* OFFICERS.)
OFFICERS: **Starhemberg! Starhemberg!**
LEOPOLD: Oh, Starhemberg, they do so love the bastard, they love the bag of bones who showed no terror, who sat out the siege when emperors fled, this moment I have dreamed of, I kneel, I kneel to thee who saved Christian Europe, I kneel and lick thy paws and here's a painter will catch my homage for all time and so on, Leopold the stooping, Leopold the supplicant!
OFFICERS: **Star — hemberg!** (STARHEMBERG *enters, goes to* LEOPOLD, *kneels.*)

Star — hemberg!

LEOPOLD: They do go on, they do adore you more than me —
STARHEMBERG: No, never —
OFFICERS: **Star — hemberg!**
LEOPOLD: **I laugh**

I laugh

I slept in lovely beds while you thrust corpses into breaches of the walls, I do most humbly thank you and of course simultaneously hate you for showing the dignity of character I was not endowed with but how was I to know the Europeans would suddenly unite? It is the first and I daresay the last occasion we have managed so fuck you and thank you! (*They embrace, swiftly, and separate.*) Now slaughter this lot. (*He indicates the* TURKISH PRISONERS.) Or their brothers back in Anatolia will say the Christians are merciful and take prisoners, no, this is a spot no Turk will stagger back to but as doormen, dustbin porters, café keepers and the like, **away**! (*The* PRISONERS *are kicked offstage.*)

I laugh
I laugh

(*To the* PAINTER.) Did you capture this? I will not embrace the mighty bonebag twice.

PAINTER: Yes —

LEOPOLD: Into Vienna now for all the sarcasm of the survivors.

STARHEMBERG: No, surely —

LEOPOLD: Yes, indeed, and if they toss cabbages —

STARHEMBERG: There are no cabbages in Vienna, we have been eating dogs —

LEOPOLD: Dogs, have you? And not the last time dogs will stand in for pastry, is the palace swept out? If so chuck the rubble back, it's right we should return to chaos, the arms askew, the monograms a shambles etcetera, and cannon holes above the bed, I think Vienna will know the crack of field guns more than once and bury babies of starvation. (*He falls, kneels, as if in a paroxysm of exhaustion. The* OFFICERS *watch, confused. The* EMPRESS *enters, gestures for them to stand away. She goes to him, rests her hands on his shoulders.*)

EMPRESS: Five hundred disembowelled women are lying in the Wienerwald.

The stench.
Of all classes.
The stench.
Of all degrees.
Islam's au revoir.
The Poles have saved Paris.

LEOPOLD: Paris...?

EMPRESS: Rome.

LEOPOLD: Rome...?

EMPRESS: London. Copenhagen. Amsterdam. The Poles have saved five million women, at this moment dreaming, knitting, wiping the arses of their infants, sucking the cocks of their husbands' friends, writing novels, hemming curtains, get up now, the wind will change and here's a cloth soaked in eau de Cologne, it has my monogram in lace which took the embroiderer twenty-seven hours, that is a waste of life some would argue, but no more fatuous than writing novels or what passes now for freedom in progressive circles and at least she has her bowels in, no Turkish dagger in her parts, get up you dear and sensitive soul, I sometimes think the barmy imaginings of the progressive rest on bayonets, do you follow? I mean the very fatuous pattering in Paris is predicated on the Poles, the spears of superstitious peasants keep their words aloft, the Turks would soon shut down their salons, in the harem with the bitches says the

Seljuk, oh, you are getting up, we have to make an entry to the city and give thanks, God knocked Allah over this time... (*She sinks down beside him.*) We have in one day an Empire back which stretches from the Alps to the Baltic, I thought, I fully thought, we would die in a seaside hotel, Leopold, kiss my ugly mouth and I'll kiss yours —

LEOPOLD: They're looking — the staff are —

EMPRESS: I do not give a piss for them, kiss me in this screaming sea, this swamp of horrid dead, we have Europe back... (*He kisses her. The* OFFICERS *draw their swords.*)

OFFICERS: **The Hapsburg! The Hapsburg!**

Scene 2

A convent. A GIRL *in a chair.*

KATRIN: In my own words. (*Pause*)

Words of my own. (*Pause*)

The poor have neither words nor drawers. (*Pause*)

Oh, for literacy, oh, for numeracy, oh, for any pack of lies! (*Pause*)

So the four soldiers said — (*Pause*)

No.

No. There may not have been four. And they may not have been soldiers. But they did have weapons and the Turk does not wear uniform so for the sake of. (*Pause*)

Let's say four. (*Pause*)

The four soldiers said lie down — well, they didn't say it, no, they did not say the words they indicated by very simple gestures this was expected of me, words were dispensed with, words were superfluous though much language was expressed on either side, by me, by them, but words not really, no. (*Pause*)

Consequently I lay my face down in the relatively sympathetic grass. **Of course I am not in the least ashamed description comes easily to me** but can I have a glass of water? The dryness of my mouth suggests anxiety but I have had a dry mouth since my throat was cut, some channel or some duct was severed, something irreparable and anatomical. (*A* NUN *places a glass of water by the chair and withdraws.*)

It's you who are ashamed not me but I forgive in all directions then one of them threw up my skirt excuse me — (*She drinks.*)

Or several of them, from now on I talk of them as plural, as many-headed, as many-legged and a mass of mouths and of course I had no drawers, to be precise — (*Pause*).

I owned a pair but for special occasions. This was indeed special but on rising in the morning I was not aware of it, and I thought many things, but first I thought — no, I exaggerate, I claim to know the order of my thoughts **what a preposterous claim** — strike that out, no, among the **cascade of impressions** — that's better — that's accurate — cascade of impressions — came the idea at least **I did not have to kiss**. (*Pause*) The lips being holy, the lips being sacred, the orifice from which I uttered my most perfect and religious thoughts only the grass would smear them but no. (*Pause*)

Can you keep up? Sometimes I find a flow and then the words go — torrent — cascade — cascade again, I used that word just now! I like that word now I have discovered it, I shall use it, probably ad nauseam, cascading! But you — (*Pause*)

And then they turned me over like a side of beef, the way the butcher flings the carcass, not without a certain familiarity, coarse-handling but with the very vaguest element of warmth, oh, no, the words are going, that isn't what I meant at all, precision is so — precision slips even as you reach for it, goes out of grasp and I was flung over and this **many mouthed thing** — (*She shudders as if taken by a fit, emitting an appalling cry and sending the water flying. The* NUN *supports her. She recovers.*)

Now I've spilled the water — don't say there's more where that came from — so it is with life — don't mop the floor, I can take it from the floor, so my mouth — (*Pause. The* NUN *withdraws.*)

My mouth which I had held to be the very shape and seat of intimacy they smothered with wet and fluid — I don't think you could call them kisses — **yes, yes, kisses, they were kisses** I try to hide behind the language, oh, the language I do twist like bars of brass to shelter in, no, they were **kisses** because a kiss can be made of hatred — kisses, yes, oh, yes... (*Pause*)

They soaked, they drenched, they swilled me with their kisses, and bruised my lips and bit my mouth and thrust these thousand tongues into my throat **and this was only the beginning only the beginning you with the book and pencil wait!** (*Pause. She controls her horror. A* PRIEST *appears from the darkness.*)

ORPHULS: I think, for today, we leave it there —

KATRIN: Why —

ORPHULS: The tension of —

KATRIN: The tension, yes —

ORPHULS: Is making you —

KATRIN: Obviously —

ORPHULS: And us for that matter, we are also —

KATRIN: You also, yes, quite rightly, suffer as I —

ORPHULS: Greatly, and —

KATRIN: Greatly, yes, why shouldn't you — (*She sees the* NUN *leave.*)

Don't go away! (*She continues her way. Pause.*)

I'm mad, aren't I? I hate the word but technically it does seem suitable. Please call me mad I wish for it. I long for madness to be ascribed to me. I thirst for such a title.

ORPHULS: I don't believe you are at all insane, only —

KATRIN: **Oh, come on!** (*With a sudden inspiration.*) Listen, this is madness, this is proof! I dream, I passionately dream, of some pretty valley in the Danube where a Muslim girl is kneeling to the East. She bows to Mecca, she spreads her Turkish things, her Turkish mirror, her Turkish mat, and threads the Transylvanian flowers through her hair when down like wind swoop Christian troopers rancid with the saddle and **stake her to the ground with knives**, her naked haunches, her perfect breasts they slash into a running sieve of blood, all channels red, all drain of horror, what satisfaction could I have from dreaming only my Turks die? No, revenge must be upon the innocent. Now, am I mad?

ORPHULS: No... (*She laughs.*)

KATRIN: I have no breasts! I have no breasts! (*She laughs and sobs.* ORPHULS *holds her in his arms. A* WOMAN *enters.*)

SUSANNAH: Is my sister there? (*The sobbing stops.*) Katrin?

ORPHULS: Yes.

SUSANNAH: It's so dark —

ORPHULS: It is dark. It must be dark.

SUSANNAH (*appearing in the shaft of light*): Yes... (*She extends a hand to* KATRIN.) Come home, now.

KATRIN: No.

SUSANNAH: Come home and —

KATRIN: **Home what's that**. (*Pause*) It's your peremptory tone I hate.

SUSANNAH: My tone's as kind as I can make it —

KATRIN: It's peremptory —

SUSANNAH: What a funny word, you do —

KATRIN: Love funny words, yes, give me a new word and I'll thank you, but home, stuff that, take home and bite it like a cold, raw egg, muck, ugh, spew, ugh, and sharp shell in the gums, no, you are peremptory and always were, beautiful, peremptory and unhappy, at least you are unhappy, thank God for that, I could like you, given time.

SUSANNAH: How much time? I carried you about, little sister.

KATRIN: I'm so cruel, aren't I? It comes of having a vocabulary and no breasts **don't touch**. (SUSANNAH *draws back.*) I can't bear to be touched now, even by those claiming pity.

SUSANNAH: I don't pity you, Katrin.

KATRIN: Why don't you? Everybody else does.

SUSANNAH: I think you are more cruel than any clot of raping mercenaries. (*Pause*) Now, you made me say that. You made me utter sentiments which in any case I do not feel. You do that to people. Let's go home.

KATRIN: I have finished with home, for which, all gratitude to Islam's infantry —
SUSANNAH: Silly —
KATRIN: **Don't call me silly in that way you do.** (*Pause*) I can't go home because — and do listen, this will be difficult for you, perhaps beyond your grasp — home is the instrument of reconciliation, the means through which all crime is rinsed in streams of sympathy and outrage doused, and blame is swallowed in upholstery, home is the suffocator of all temper, the place where the preposterous becomes the tolerable and hell itself is stacked on shelves, I wish to hold on to my agony, it's all I have. (*Pause*)
SUSANNAH: I had such a pleasant room prepared for you...
KATRIN: Use it to fuck in. (*She bursts out.*) Oh, I am unforgivable! I only said that because he is here! (*Pause*) But do, do use it for love, you drive men mad, you know you do. (*She looks at* ORPHULS.) She does. Their eyes go fixed. (*She turns to go.*)
SUSANNAH: Where will you go, then?
KATRIN: With the nuns, like any vagrant. (*She goes out. Pause.*)
ORPHULS: She is — she boils and fumes — she —
SUSANNAH: She always did. Her ordeal has made no difference. And of course, I hate her, too.
ORPHULS: Then why do you —
SUSANNAH: I don't know. We often choose to live with those we hate, so I observe. And those we think we love, we soon grow to hate. I exaggerate, of course, it is the effect of being with a priest in a dark room. There is no bread in the city. Have you any? I am starving. (*Pause. He looks at her.*) Turkish carpets and whole tents are being swopped for single cabbages, would you believe? (*She exposes her breast to him.*) Come on, the next thing will be an epidemic and we'll all be dead by Christmas.
ORPHULS (*turning away his face*): I should love nothing more than that, but I've no bread.
SUSANNAH: Chocolate, then?
ORPHULS: No...(*She covers her breast.*) What I would not give for a piece of chocolate now...
SUSANNAH: I know.
ORPHULS: All the chocolate one eats, and now —
SUSANNAH: It's the way, isn't it, of all things? But the Emperor's back and they don't appear without the kitchens, why are you interrogating my sister?
ORPHULS: We are recording all — God forgive me, I would die for a loaf now —
SUSANNAH: I understand, but —
ORPHULS: We are keeping testimony of the passage of Islam, I am commissioned by the See, Oh, God, give me a loaf, somebody, it is a sacred obligation to our people, anyway it is not an interrogation, she is under no compulsion, would you please leave now, you are subjecting me to terrible anxiety, how could I look at you again in

times of plenty knowing I might have —

SUSANNAH: You may come to me and ask me, pay me the conventional attentions and if I am not otherwise engaged, who knows, I —

ORPHULS: Conventional attentions?

SUSANNAH: Yes, manners will be back as soon as the shops are open. (*She smiles.*) I am most dreadfully hungry. (*She pulls her clothing closer, goes to leave, stops.*) Obviously, you wouldn't have a loaf, would you? You would have given it away. (*Pause. They look at one another.*)

ORPHULS: Had I a single slice, I should pass by the dying and not show it. (*Pause. She turns, but at this moment, a small loaf is thrown from the darkness. It lands at* ORPHULS's *feet. Both he and* SUSANNAH *go to grab it, but he is the swifter. Undoing her dress, she steps into the darkness. Pause, then he follows. After some moments,a* HOODED FIGURE *appears in the shaft of light. Pause. The sound of* SUSANNAH's *receding footsteps on the stone floor.* ORPHULS *appears. He looks at the* FIGURE.) Who the — who the fuck are — (*He tears off his hood. It is* STARHEMBERG.) Oh, fuck, it is the man who saved Vienna... (*He kneels at his feet.*) I am a most ambitious priest and love God, I assure you, in the heat of her sweltering...

STARHEMBERG: Excellent.

ORPHULS: But you...?

STARHEMBERG: Me? I listen.

ORPHULS: And do you creep in many rooms? I only ask? I kiss your feet who saved a million souls, why do you listen to girls' miseries? Inform me, I am your servant and no matter what the sins I absolve you, I would be skewered on Islamic daggers but for you, make me your Confessor, I would be honoured not only to hear but share your pains. And thank you for the bun, I was in hell there. (*Pause.* STARHEMBERG *raises him, kisses him, and goes out.*)

Scene 3

A palace. COURTIERS. *A chair.* LEOPOLD *enters. He topples the chair and perches on the result. They shift uncomfortably.*

LEOPOLD: Sometimes, you will want to laugh. And you will feel, no, I must not laugh. Sometimes you will suffer the embarassment of one who feels exposed to an obnoxious privacy. You will feel, he should never have shown me that. And sometimes you will experience the terrible nausea that accompanies an idiocy performed by one for whom you felt respect. As if the world had lost its balance. I can only tell you, all these feelings I permit. So laugh when the urge seizes you, and then, be ashamed of the laugh. The Emperor only acts the insecurity of all order. Do you accept the truth of that? (*They shift uncomfortably.*) No one understands! Nihil comprehensa! Now, you may turn the chair up. (*The chair is put on its legs* LEOPOLD *sprawls.*)

IPSTEIN: Morality.

LEOPOLD: Mm.

IPSTEIN: Has utterly collapsed.

LEOPOLD: It does in sieges. Like cakes left in the rain. And humour also, that deteriorates. The sort of joke you would not twitch a muscle for in peacetime sets crowds of starving rocking in a siege.

IPSTEIN: Humour I think, we can leave aside for —

LEOPOLD: **Why leave humour out**! (*Pause.* IPSTEIN *shrugs.*) Do I bully you? Don't shudder, no one will hack your hand off, this is not Rome or Russia.

HARDENSTEIN: Women are selling themselves and the bourgeoises are the worst.

LEOPOLD: You should pity the priveliged, how they suffer in adversity. See the best shops are stocked first. Next.

FALLENGOTT: The currency is unstable.

LEOPOLD: The currency is always unstable.

FALLENGOTT: Not like this.

LEOPOLD: I am sick of currency and its instability. I shrink to think a single life, a dog's or pigeon's even, should be warped by currency and its antics. Hang currency from trees.

FALLENGOTT: We might as well, it is that useless.

LEOPOLD: I sense the coinage has found a friend in you.

FALLENGOTT: Not a bit, but —

LEOPOLD: **Off your knees to coins**, it is a despicable sight. Are the bankers back yet?

HARDENSTEIN: The Jews never left.

LEOPOLD: The fall of shells is like a passing shower to them. Where is the Turkish treasure?

FALLENGOTT: Lying in ravines.

LEOPOLD: Then float the new economy on that. Enough, and thank you for your opinions, I weigh them all, I seem brusque, I seem shallow but in privacy I meditate profoundly, you must take that on trust, of course. (*They start to leave.* LEOPOLD *places his hand on the* PAINTER's *sleeve.*) Not you. (*The* COURTIERS *depart. Pause.*) I speak everything, like one variety of idiot. And you are silent, like the other. Draw me now. I pose. (*He kneels on the floor like a dog.*) I pose. And thus cheat your imagination.

PAINTER (*turning to a fresh page*): How?

LEOPOLD: Because the artist hopes his portrait shows a secret truth, and I show my secret. Call this 'He Comes Back to Vienna'.

PAINTER: Must I?

LEOPOLD: Yes. (*He begins drawing.*)

PAINTER: I think, by discarding the formality of monarchy, you think you disrupt criticism, and by playing the fool, disarm any who would dare call you so, and thereby flatter your intelligence. I hope I am not offending you.

LEOPOLD: You were never this perceptive on the battlefield.

PAINTER: I was too cold.

LEOPOLD: **It is cold, this is Europe**...!

PAINTER: Yes... yes... so you said... at every foggy ditch and burial — (*He throws down the book.*) It's — really it's — impossible! You cannot — an artist cannot hope to paint an act! Find another — find a —

LEOPOLD (*abandoning his absurd pose, and sitting on the floor*): No, no, you are the one... you are... (*Pause. He is weeping.* STARHEMBERG *enters, looks at them.*) I'm crying again... Starhemberg... crying again... (STARHEMBERG *goes to him, cradles his head.*) Why? Why this weeping all the time? (*The* PAINTER *sketches this, furtively.*) Don't you weep? You don't, do you? **Why is it, then, it infuriates me** — (*The* PAINTER *goes to leave discreetly.*) Don't slip away with that! (*He stops.*) Show me the book. (*He offers the book.*) You see, he gets it down, the moment of despair, his fingers work like lightning to capture that, how well he seizes that — (*He tears out the page, gives the book back. The* PAINTER *leaves.*) Where do you go at nights? You are unobtainable.

STARHEMBERG: Am I not free? I have no titles which are not honorary now.

LEOPOLD: No, none, and at your own request. But half the time you are not in your premises, and the messengers say the state of the windows suggests the genius has quit. Four times I have left messages. You are a hero and yet you creep around in hats, we need our hero, we are afraid you will be discovered lying in some alley and then the word will go around Starhemberg is out of favour, there's gratitude for you, when nothing could be further from the truth!

STARHEMBERG: During the siege I had half the cannon turned to face in.

LEOPOLD: In? Why in?

STARHEMBERG: Every night a dozen citizens slipped out with handkerchiefs on which were written **we love Islam** in misshapen Arab script. I must tell you, at the lowest point I received a delegation who proposed the burning of all effigies of Christ, and as for the Imperial standard, I saw it stuffed inside a drain-pipe. Officers were tearing off their epaulets, and priests lurked in wigs. I forced freedom on them, and when they applaud me, their claps are drowning out the shame which roars inside their ears. I loathe the crowd. I love big hats.

LEOPOLD: They are only frail... they are only frail... I cannot criticize them... how can I, the arch-deserter, criticize? You must help us to restore ourselves. Be a mirror in which we dwarves may see the possibility of godlike self.

STARHEMBERG: No.

LEOPOLD: Restore us, Starhemberg, who has no flaws — (STARHEMBERG *turns to leave*.) **Who said yer can go!** (*He stops*.) I think you are a selfish and self-loving fantasist or you would have surrendered months ago. (*Pause*) No, no, listen, I owe you everything and don't despise me, I can have you made a saint, do you want to be a saint? It can be done, the long grey jaw and hooded eye, excellent, try that if you are tired of soldiering, but not this anonymity, or do you hate us? (*Pause*) You do... so that's your burden... you are thin with hate... Oh, Starhemberg, you are crueller than the worst Arab butcher, who stabs with childlike relish and then grows tired, and waking in the morning, plays with the infants he forgot to slay. Starhemberg, my maker, you are ill... (*He goes to him, holds him*.)

STARHEMBERG: The innocent are not innocent...

LEOPOLD: **I laugh! I laugh!**

EMPRESS (*entering*): Starhemberg! How rarely he! Oh, his unfamiliar! Kiss me, then! (*He kisses her hand*.) Cold mouth. Have you a mistress?

STARHEMBERG: I love a woman.

EMPRESS: But your mouth is cold!

LEOPOLD: He holds us all in spite.

EMPRESS: Not me.

LEOPOLD: Yes, you included! Someone is writing his biography, but he will give no evidence. And the city architect has sculpted him for Starhemberg Square, but without a face! It is ridiculous, when can he do the face?

STARHEMBERG: Let it have no face.

LEOPOLD: **I laugh. I laugh.**

EMPRESS: Are you loyal to the Hapsburgs?

STARHEMBERG: I can conceive of no improvement in the nature of the government.

LEOPOLD: You see! That is how he is!

EMPRESS (*looking at Starhemberg*): He thinks his boldness will win our admiration. He is very near offence, and thinks we will admire his subtlety. I do admire it, so there! Do sit, or won't you?

STARHEMBERG: No.

EMPRESS: Of course not! To sit would end his condescension, I do admire all your moves, I think you are a cold and wonderfully imagined man, I mean, you are your own invention, isn't that so?

LEOPOLD: My wife is so perceptive, her gaze melts snow.

STARHEMBERG: Yes.

EMPRESS: There you are! And a reply of one syllable, for more would only spoil the effect. I feel such attraction for you, Starhemberg, I would run away with you to a pigman's hut and fuck the rest of my existence out!

LEOPOLD: **I laugh**!

EMPRESS: You see, I can match all your gestures. No real man is worth the effort, but one who invents, and re-invents himself! He can keep us heated!

LEOPOLD: **I laugh**!

EMPRESS (*to* LEOPOLD): As you do, as you also do... (*She kisses* LEOPOLD.) Starhemberg, we must invent the European now, from broken bits. Glue head to womb and so on. And fasten hair to cracked, mad craniums. And stop being ashamed. Now, go, you excellent actor, do go... (*He bows.)*

Scene 4

An Institute of Science. A semi-circle of PHYSICIANS. KATRIN *naked to the waist.* SUSANNAH *and* STARHEMBERG *in the audience.*

GRUNDFELT: She is nineteen. She is from the agricultural district of Thuringia. She is one of nine children. She is literate. She suffered on the twenty-third of August. She was without benefit of surgeons. She is pregnant and in the fourth month of her term. She gave testimony to the Bishop's Commission on Atrocity.

KATRIN: I volunteer my disfigurement.

GRUNDFELT: She comes of her own free will.

KATRIN: I needed no persuasion.

GRUNDFELT: She welcomes the scrutiny of the Institute.

KATRIN: I welcome it.

GRUNDFELT: We are grateful to this courageous and patriotic woman.

KATRIN: And I am grateful to you.

GRUNDFELT: Drawing is permitted. (*The* AUDIENCE *rises and surrounds* KATRIN, *with books and pencils*.)

STARHEMBERG: They cluster her... How thick they are on her, and urgent...

SUSANNAH: Are you a surgeon? Hurry along with your pencil or you will miss the itemizing of the wounds.

STARHEMBERG: I shall see her...

SUSANNAH: Everyone will see her. She is determined her misery will go into print, and colour, too, you are staring at me in a way which at one time would have been thought offensive...

STARHEMBERG: Her absent breasts, and yours so very present...

SUSANNAH: It is peculiar, we would have thought at one time, to have such intellectual symposia among men who cannot muster a sandwich between them....

STARHEMBERG: Your succulence, and her aridity...
SUSANNAH: But we swiftly become used to anything, don't you find? All right, what have you got? I don't want pig fat, oh, God, you are Starhemberg —
STARHEMBERG: Introduce me to her.
SUSANNAH: Aren't you, you are Starhemberg, I am bathed in confusion —
STARHEMBERG: You honour me quite unnecessarily —
SUSANNAH: I bite my words —
STARHEMBERG: The world has dropped several rungs, and us with it, when will you speak to her?
SUSANNAH: Now, if you command it —
STARHEMBERG: I command nothing any more — (*She turns to go.*) Wait — I also love women —
SUSANNAH: What are you asking me?
STARHEMBERG: On the floor here, show me —
SUSANNAH: Show you?
STARHEMBERG: I have seen you fucked —
SUSANNAH: Impossible —
STARHEMBERG: No, it's so — go down and let me look at you — your hair — your crevices —
SUSANNAH: I prefer we —
STARHEMBERG: I only ask to gaze, there's no complication —
SUSANNAH: I must, since you saved Vienna. (*She lies down among the benches, draws up her skirts. The voice of* GRUNDFELT *drones.* STARHEMBERG *stares down at her, and up occasionally.*)
STARHEMBERG: Up now, they're quitting — (*She rises again, straightening her skirt.*) Introduce me, then wait in the Ballgasse. (*She makes her way to the front.*)
GRUNDFELT: Our feelings of sympathy are not less profound for the objectivity we have attempted here in detailing your condition —
OTHERS: Hear, hear —
KATRIN: Nor is my modesty less whole for the intensity of your examination —
OTHERS: Hear, hear —
GRUNDFELT: We thank you both for this and for your gracious manner.
KATRIN: I thank you equally, shall this be printed and in colour? (*They hesitate.*)
BRUSTEIN: At this moment we had only thought to record your terrible misfortune for the archive of the Institute...
KATRIN: Oh, no, I understood there was a publication —
BRUSTEIN: In learned journals, some details might —
KATRIN: No, no, but in the shops, I mean —
BRUSTEIN: I — did we —
KATRIN: Oh, certainly!
GRUNDFELT: I have no recollection we —
KATRIN: Assuredly, some six thousand copies!

GRUNDFELT: I don't think any —
KATRIN: **Yes, six thousand**. I don't dream these figures. They printed fifteen thousand of Duke Starhemberg, he hangs in every pub, and eighteen thousand of the Emperor, why not, there is a vast supply of cartridge in the city, and ink's no problem, some have taken to drinking it —
SUSANNAH (*advancing with a shawl*): My sister is —
KATRIN: **Nothing**. My sister is. (*Pause*)
STARHEMBERG (*walking down*): Is there a drawing?
PAINTER: A preliminary sketch —
STARHEMBERG: Then tint it, and add her face.
SUSANNAH: My sister is —
KATRIN: Nothing. My sister is. Do arrange and hurry with the proofs. If you have not my face, I'll sit here longer.
PAINTER: If the Duke commissions this, I —
KATRIN: What duke? It's me has all the copyright.
STARHEMBERG: Please, ask her to be covered... (*Pause.* KATRIN *allows* SUSANNAH *to draw a shawl over her naked shoulders.* STARHEMBERG *goes to the front.*) Arrange a sitting. She is staying in a convent.
KATRIN: And another, later, like this...! (*She pretends to feed a child.*) I raise my infant, who is crying for his feed, but to the absent breasts, where no milk flows! His arms reach out, his tiny hands... ! Imagine my expression! Imagine his!
STARHEMBERG: Sketch as she says.
KATRIN: Ten thousand copies.
GRUNDFELT: I doubt this would achieve a sale of tens —
KATRIN: **You misjudge**. (*Pause*) And if they don't, then post them through the doors... (GRUNDFELT *bows, withdraws, with the* PHYSICIANS.)
SUSANNAH: This is Duke Starhemberg. (KATRIN *looks at him.*)
KATRIN: The birth is for the seventeenth. I want it public in the square, and banks of seats. No awnings, even if it rains, and let actresses be midwives if nurses have their scruples. (*To* STARHEMBERG.) Why would you not look at me?
STARHEMBERG: I only look when I am certain I shall see.
KATRIN: You will see. (*She gets up, falls against* SUSANNAH, *who holds her. With an effort of will,* KATRIN *rids herself of* SUSANNAH.) Oh, you all so want me to be spoiled! Kiss me! (SUSANNAH *goes to kiss her.* KATRIN *removes her cheek.*) I don't trust kisses! Embrace me! (SUSANNAH *goes to hold her, she arches away.*) I suffocate! You only rub your grief against my flesh, as if it would come off, as a cow will back itself against the thorn and scrape its hide. That's how we kiss, that's how we hold! Where is my nun, I want to go now, Mother! (*She pulls on a gown.*) This was no endurance, do you know why? None would look me in the eye, and I have such lovely eyes. Are my eyes so dangerous? No Turk did either. (*The* NUN *enters.*) My eyes remain unravished,

Mother, like unentered rooms... (*The* NUN *encloses her, leads her to the door.* ORPHULS *enters, bows to her.*)

STARHEMBERG: Let me father your child... (*Pause.* KATRIN *stops.*)

KATRIN: But it won't live! (*She goes out. Pause.*)

SUSANNAH: I think we live in Hell, but something makes Hell tolerable. What is it? Anger? I am so bad at anger.

ORPHULS: This is not Hell.

SUSANNAH: Not Hell? What's Hell, then?

ORPHULS: Absence.

SUSANNAH: I assure you, this is absence.

ORPHULS: Of God. (*Pause*)

SUSANNAH (*to* STARHEMBERG): Take me to the café. You said you would, for showing you God's absence... (*She goes out.*)

ORPHULS: The siege was simultaneously a moment of degeneracy and of the highest moral order. On the one hand, every fence to immorality was torn down, and on the other, peculiar sacrifices were made in the spirit of human love. Did you find this? (STARHEMBERG *does not reply.*) Every morning when we awoke, we felt the possibility of **utter transformation**, rising with the sun. Death, obviously, but worse, enslavement to all things foreign... the crying of the mullahs in their tents... shall we never hear again the crying of the mullahs in their tents? How tightly I did hold the woman's arse to me, her warmth, our miserable thin blanket and I kissed her hollowed neck with tears all down my face, **ring the bells I said, where are our bells today**? And then at last, the bells crashed back, drowning, waves of drowning, seas of booming iron, and she stirred slowly, some widow, some pale, inconsequential widow who held in her thin body all that was ours, all culture, all effigy in her broken lips. We pulled on our drawers under the dirty sheets, ice on the windows, and on the table, last night's greasy plate...

STARHEMBERG: Hearing you I know I could only love a corrupt priest...

ORPHULS: Don't betray me. I am ambitious.

STARHEMBERG: Never.

ORPHULS: Once you were seen in every street, on every barricade, I heard people swear you had been seen in seven quarters simultaneously, and though I never saw you, I imagined I did, and children pointed to your profile in the clouds and said I know that beak... !'

STARHEMBERG: I love the plumpness of your face. I know when you serve mass, you rarely think of Christ.

ORPHULS: I think of Him, but — (*Pause*) No, I hardly think of Christ, rather, I think — I am Him.

STARHEMBERG: Yes...

ORPHULS: I tell you this! I tell you, God knows why, why do I tell you? Don't betray me, I am so ambitious!

STARHEMBERG: I would rather take your blessing than a thousand cardinals stinking of celibacy shook their absolution over me. (*An old* WOMAN *enters*.)

FIRST MOTHER: Is it him? Is it his voice crying love?

ORPHULS: No.

FIRST MOTHER: I find him everywhere!

STARHEMBERG: Yes, he is an itinerant priest. (*He goes out*.)

FIRST MOTHER: His long words, his lovely words, all his lovely education licks the ceiling and —

ORPHULS: I've no more bread. (*Pause*)
I mean —
I have a bit but —
I need that for —
Oh, fuck you, take it! (*He pulls some bread from under his cassock*.)

FIRST MOTHER (*taking it*): Don't swear so, you'll make enemies.

ORPHULS: I have only one enemy and that is you. I take that back.

FIRST MOTHER: You take everything back but only after you've said it.

ORPHULS: I hope you will not eat that here, it scalds my soul to think I might have fucked a woman for it and all it does is extend your burdensome life, I take that back, but you know what I mean.

FIRST MOTHER: I wouldn't burden you if your sisters were more like daughters.

ORPHULS: You have a miraculous appetite and thrive on bird shit. Most of the old collapsed and died in the first month of the siege. I looked in all their faces, but where were you? Take her swift, I prayed to God, but no, claw at the door before the morning guns...

FIRST MOTHER: You love me, that's what kept me whole.

ORPHULS: So you say.

FIRST MOTHER: You must do or you wouldn't tolerate me. You are kind and I am so demanding, you are busy and I pester you —

ORPHULS: Yes, well, I —

FIRST MOTHER: Oh, yes, but I shall be no trouble to you soon, my life's as good as chucked —

ORPHULS: So you keep on saying, but —

FIRST MOTHER: I live for you —

ORPHULS: For me, but —

FIRST MOTHER: My little one —

ORPHULS: Oh, God in Heaven —

FIRST MOTHER: His tiny arms went round me once, he hid his darling face in my poor skirt —

ORPHULS: **Please! oh, please**! (*She is silent. She chews bread. Pause*.) I try, I do try, to eradicate you from my life, to erase you, every morning like a butcher rubbing down his bench...

FIRST MOTHER: Too deep a groove... (*He nods*.)
Too deep a stain... (*He turns his back. Pause*.)
Mind all these women.

ORPHULS: Yes. (*She starts to move away, stops*.)

FIRST MOTHER: I see you in that bishop's hat.
ORPHULS: You always did. Since I first joined the choir.
FIRST MOTHER: My son, almighty in his bishop's hat —
ORPHULS: **If I want to be a bishop I'll decide.**
FIRST MOTHER: Of course you will.
ORPHULS: I am not ambitious. It is you who is ambitious. Sickeningly so. I am happy as a pastor here. Happy and fulfilled.
FIRST MOTHER: Good. I won't keep you, then. You must have such a lot to do —
ORPHULS: Stay as long as you like, I — stay if you —
FIRST MOTHER: No, I must get on —
ORPHULS: Must you? Well, if you must, you —
FIRST MOTHER: Don't grieve for me.
ORPHULS: **You talk about dying all the time but do you!**
FIRST MOTHER (*with infinite patience*): You will, of course. You will grieve for me.
ORPHULS: I hate the way you eat. Half the crumbs are on the floor.
FIRST MOTHER: Always ate this way.
ORPHULS: I know and it always horrified me.
FIRST MOTHER: I thought you liked the common people. We are common —
ORPHULS: **Sometimes I think I could murder you.**
FIRST MOTHER (*kneeling, brushing up the crumbs*): I know. It's love.
ORPHULS: Stop that! Get up! (*She finishes, gets up.*) Go away, now.
FIRST MOTHER (*looking at him*): My own son. (*She goes out. Pause.*)
ORPHULS: I love you! I do love you! (*Pause*) If everything remains the same, why did we suffer? I buried thirty in a day and still I imitate! (*He examines himself.*) Other self. Other self unborn. Wrist inside my wrist. Lung inside my lung. (*Pause*) And in the hospitals they said — the young but not only the young — the injustice of my death so sours me, I have not been, I have not been yet what I might have been. But looking at them I thought, had you been, what would you have been? What magnificence? And I concluded, none. A gift of years they would have squandered in casual repetition and in servile acts. Clay, therefore. Complaining clay. (*He looks aside, sees* SUSANNAH, *who has returned, watching him.*)
SUSANNAH: Do you talk to yourself? Another madman of the siege? (*Pause*) You blush! Wonderful blush!
ORPHULS: I was — I was —
SUSANNAH: Praying?
ORPHULS: Not praying, no. (*Pause. He looks at her.*) I have no bread today.
SUSANNAH: I've eaten.

ORPHULS: Eaten? Oh... (*Pause. Then with immense will.*) Be my mistress, then. (*A prolonged pause.*)
SUSANNAH: Yes.
ORPHULS: Oh, my own bitch, yes...! (*She goes towards him. He recoils.*) No.
SUSANNAH (*stopped*): No?
ORPHULS: You must not — simply —
SUSANNAH: No —
ORPHULS: Do you understand? Not simply, but —
SUSANNAH: Yes. (*Pause*)
ORPHULS: Suffer. (*Pause*)
It. (*She goes out. He collapses to the floor, a ball of ecstasy.*)

Scene 5

A cellar in Vienna. STARHEMBERG *among the* OUTCASTS.

STARHEMBERG: In all calamity, the persistence of the destitute! In all catastrophe, the resilience of the poor! The tolerant, the semi-tolerant, **crushed to death**! The educated, the semi-educated, **trod to dust**! The cruel, the semi-cruel, **scorched to ashes**, but the carriers of neither hope nor property, **they shall inherit the earth**! That's you! (*He holds one tightly.*) Who are your true loves, those who drop small coins in your paw?
FIRST BEGGAR: No —
STARHEMBERG: No — those who come with leaflets preaching revolution?
FIRST BEGGAR: No —
STARHEMBERG: No — those who offer beds at Christmas, do you love those?
FIRST BEGGAR: No —
STARHEMBERG: No, the ones who drive their iron wheels over your splitting shins, they are your brothers!
FIRST BEGGAR: I don't see what —
STARHEMBERG: **Yes, the fraternity of bastardy**! (*He releases him.*) Yes, very few of you died, I notice, my dear friends, very few, oh, very few, and had Islam burst the gates they would not have stooped to hack your noses, those who have some gristle left, no, the beggar attracts so little violence, we must learn from him **don't stand behind me I hate that** do I lecture you, I don't mean to, I am in search of education, I clown, I misinform, I lick the oily effusion that trickles from your gut **don't come up behind me** —

SECOND BEGGAR: You are a mad and vicious fucker, Starhemberg —

STARHEMBERG: **Don't come up behind me I love to see your face in** which is written **survival of the fittest**, up you monarch! (*He hoists the* BEGGAR *onto his back, and parades with him*.) I am the horse to him! Spur me, you cannibal! Whip me, you angel!

SECOND BEGGAR: Put us down, yer cunt...!

STARHEMBERG: **I caught him with his gob in the corpse's belly**!

SECOND BEGGAR: Fuck off, you mouth and arsehole bastard —

STARHEMBERG: I did! And excellent! Withold respect? Not me! I canter, I perform my dressage, I am as perfect as the carriage horse, the hearse animal, oh, master, oh, genius in self-perpetuation, **I caught him with his gob in the entrails**!

SECOND BEGGAR: Who the fuck are —

STARHEMBERG: **Not you? Then it was your double**!

SECOND BEGGAR: Down or I'll kick the kidneys out yer arse —

STARHEMBERG: Down? To the humble soil? Tread pavements, you? Oh, no, not you, **Monarch**! (*He tips him brutally to the floor*.)

FIRST WOMAN BEGGAR: You should watch it, how you hurt the feelings of these gentlemen.

STARHEMBERG (*sitting*): Their sensitivity engulfs me.

FIRST WOMAN BEGGAR: They also breathe.

STARHEMBERG: Yes, I smell it.

FIRST WOMAN BEGGAR: They also suffer.

STARHEMBERG: What, the indigestion caused by human meat? No, I bow to such persistence, you know I do, I am your student, I am your novice, and my tongue hangs out to the dribble of your wit like the putti in the fountain, piss your life to me, I drink!

SECOND WOMAN BEGGAR: You are no fucking angel —

STARHEMBERG: No angel yet — but trying —

SECOND WOMAN BEGGAR: **Who fed you**?

STARHEMBERG: The army commissariat.

SECOND WOMAN BEGGAR: **I spit on that**.

STARHEMBERG: I feel your spit, a cool and perfect fluid...

FIRST WOMAN BEGGAR: Why do you come down here?

STARHEMBERG: To swim your gratitude! To bathe in your eternal thanks, why else? What's the gift of monarchy to your applause? The gratitude of wealth is pure selfishness, but those who only own the gutter, to be praised by them! (*He mockingly cups his ear*.)

Deliverer, did you say?
Redeemer, over there?
No, didn't catch it, so deafening is the accolade
— (*He fondles the* FIRST WOMAN BEGGAR.)
Fuck with me, I'll kiss your scabs, I'll be a Christ
to you, an ageing Christ who slipped the crucifixion —

FIRST WOMAN BEGGAR: Oh, slag yerself, I done with rubbing —

STARHEMBERG: Rubbing, she calls love...!

SECOND BEGGAR (*threatening him closely*): Nothing fills me with more violence, mister, than a punctured snob who spunks from squalor —

STARHEMBERG: He identifies me —

SECOND BEGGAR: Lock yer gob, you shit picnic —

STARHEMBERG: How my lip swells from your compliments — (SECOND BEGGAR *goes to attack* STARHEMBERG, *but* STARHEMBERG *is the swifter and takes the* BEGGAR *in a terrible embrace*.) Oh, dance you terrible hater, dance, sick-with-life, **not dancing**! (*He jerks the* BEGGAR.) Oh, he shifts in some gavotte, some mockery of civil manners, teach me, I can't follow — (*He jerks him again*.) Oh, your movements, are these the **veiled messages of love** —

SECOND BEGGAR: You — hurt — you —

STARHEMBERG: Or symbols of the hierarchy? I can't imitate!

SECOND BEGGAR: Oh — fuck and —

STARHEMBERG (*lowering him in a hold*): Down now, piss-odour, to your loved level... (*He pushes his mouth to the flagstones. A silence. He releases him, moves away, shuddering*.)

THIRD BEGGAR: You will end up eye-gouged, or nose-spiked, I dare suggest, the wretched harbour grievances, having little else to harbour... (STARHEMBERG *looks at him*.) I think it possible we are related...

STARHEMBERG: So's all humanity, if we could excavate the bedrooms.

THIRD BEGGAR: Touché, but I am an Esterhazy of the excluded line.

STARHEMBERG: I knew the nose.

THIRD BEGGAR: I am not after favours, have you seen my sister, I am not after favours, obviously, she was put in the assylum at Estragom —

STARHEMBERG: Go away, now —

THIRD BEGGAR: In a room, and chained, how could she write poetry in such a posture, the manacles were bolted to the ceiling, impossible I should have thought, she was committed for no other reason than her poetry, it did not rhyme, you see, I ask no favours, why have they dimmed, your eyes? (*He sits at* STARHEMBERG's *feet, silent*.)

FIRST WOMAN BEGGAR: You have hurt Larry's throat, you mad cat...

STARHEMBERG: Then he can shake his bowl for two defects instead of one.

FIRST WOMAN BEGGAR: You are a proper pig melt in this mood...

SECOND BEGGAR (*roaring at a distance*): **I will blind 'is eyes**!

BEGGARS: Down, Larry, down, son...

SECOND BEGGAR: **Blind 'im, everyone**!

STARHEMBERG: You could not blind a pigeon if it sat trussed in your fingers...

SECOND BEGGAR: **Piss in yer mouth**!

BEGGARS: Steady, Larry...
SECOND WOMAN BEGGAR: 'ho asked you here in any case?
STARHEMBERG: Nobody asked, you once perfect, breath-stopping excellence — for whom I once would have crawled whole avenues of rotting butchery...
SECOND WOMAN BEGGAR: Piss in yer mouth.
STARHEMBERG: So you say.
FOURTH BEGGAR (*sitting by* STARHEMBERG): You know, so tell me, shall there ever be a system with no poor?
STARHEMBERG: Never. Unless they gaol the poor in palaces. I don't rule that out.
FOURTH BEGGAR: And shall the poor men burn the rich men's houses?
STARHEMBERG: Yes, again, and again, or how else could the rich feel happy?
FOURTH BEGGAR: I follow nothing 'e says! Nothing!
SECOND BEGGAR: **Poke 'im in the eyeballs, then!**
FOURTH BEGGAR: **Shuddup!**
STARHEMBERG (*grabing the* FOURTH BEGGAR *by the collar*): Describe what hope you have, your hope, what is it?
FOURTH BEGGAR: Hope?
STARHEMBERG: Yes, you know the stuff, it came in with the mother's milk, had you no mother?
FOURTH BEGGAR: Yes —
STARHEMBERG: What, then? (*Pause*)
FOURTH BEGGAR: Dinner!
STARHEMBERG: **No, after dinner**! (*Pause*)
FOURTH BEGGAR: None, after dinner... (STARHEMBERG *gets up*.)
FIRST WOMAN BEGGAR: I don't think you should visit us. Let us be vicious, as we are, and you be vicious, as you are, and piss in all mouths, but no trespass. (*Pause.* STARHEMBERG *starts to go*.)
FOURTH BEGGAR: Take me...! (*He stops, looks at the* FOURTH BEGGAR, *shakes his head, goes out.* The FOURTH BEGGAR *rushes after him*.)

Scene 6

A darkened room. An arid and dusty old WOMAN *in a chair.* STARHEMBERG *enters.*

SECOND MOTHER: Why are you here?
STARHEMBERG: God knows.

SECOND MOTHER: Here again, and don't know why. Dux. Imperator. Have you aged?
STARHEMBERG: Yes.
SECOND MOTHER: Deliverer. Defender. One day you will enter and I shan't be here. A woman with a baby will be here, and the shutters open, all sunlight and diapers.
STARHEMBERG: Obviously.
SECOND MOTHER: I have nothing more to say and you keep coming here.
STARHEMBERG: Yes.
SECOND MOTHER: Do you love me so much?
STARHEMBERG: It would appear so.
SECOND MOTHER: It would. Tribune. Liberator.
STARHEMBERG: Once I saw you naked. But only once.
SECOND MOTHER: You want to talk of these things, but I have nothing to say.
STARHEMBERG: You have nothing to say but I have much to ask.
SECOND MOTHER: Speak your questions to my grave.
STARHEMBERG: I will do.
SECOND MOTHER: Why do I need to hear?
STARHEMBERG: I would have been your child. How I lay and wished I was your child. If I had been your child none of this would be necessary.
SECOND MOTHER: Generalissimus, you cannot know how tired I am.
STARHEMBERG: I also. And your breasts were like the breasts of a witch.
SECOND MOTHER: Is that the mid-day bell?
STARHEMBERG: The antithesis of sculpture.
SECOND MOTHER: It is. And now I wind my watch.
STARHEMBERG: The antithesis of abundance.
SECOND MOTHER: Thus is my day divided. Only at night do I open the shutter. On the eight o'clock bell. Thus is my day divided.
STARHEMBERG: I come as rarely as I can. Often I wish to come, and refuse myself.
SECOND MOTHER: Yes, rarely, Gloriosus Austriae.
STARHEMBERG: Naked, only once, and I believe you knew that I was there.
SECOND MOTHER: My teeth are falling.
STARHEMBERG: Mine also.
SECOND MOTHER: Sometimes I hear a tinkle as one strikes the tiles. I have been asleep and open-mouthed. The saliva stains my shoulder. My head goes always to the left.
STARHEMBERG: I came behind you and —
SECOND MOTHER: So the left collar of my dress is pale.
STARHEMBERG: I must come here all the same. (*He sits. A long silence. He rocks, head in hands.*)

SECOND MOTHER: Oh, my darling one, oh, my little son, my darling one... (*A long pause.*)
STARHEMBERG: Do they bring you food?
SECOND MOTHER: At one.
STARHEMBERG: Eat, then. Do eat.
SECOND MOTHER: Why? (*He shrugs.*)
STARHEMBERG: Cease eating, then. And my visits could cease, too.
SECOND MOTHER: Deus Imperator. My lip is thin as paper and it spontaneously bleeds... (*He rises to his feet.*)
Deus...
Deus... (*He goes to her. The interruption of a loud voice on the stairs.*)
EMPRESS: **Le sixième étage**! (*Footsteps on the boards.*)
This is her room! (*The door opens.*)
I enter! I burst in! A clumsy and unwelcome mound of governing flesh!
Lights!
Open the shutters! (*A servant enters.*)
Is she here? I did not knock, I might surprise her straddling the commode, but I am a woman of the world and more, where are you, Mother of Deliverance? And why this hatred of la clarté, das licht, are you afraid to witness your own decay? (*The* SERVANT *throws back the shutters.*) I understand, I also have abolished mirrors and am half your age — (*The light shows* STARHEMBERG *and the* SECOND MOTHER. *The* EMPRESS *stops.*) Starhemberg. The filial obligation. (*Pause. She bows to the* SECOND MOTHER.) Madam, you have more magnetism for this man than all five hundred rooms of the Kaiserhof. I think your son is a remarkable swine.
SECOND MOTHER: He is not my son. I never suffered him, nor any other infant.
EMPRESS: The light is cruel... does no one sweep in here? My shoes crack biscuits and the skeletons of gorged mice... it is a proper kaiserhof of rodents and merciless to the nostrils, leave the door wide, je souffre, ich ersticke. (*To* STARHEMBERG.) Why are you here, I am embarassed.
STARHEMBERG: I don't know.
EMPRESS: And why am I, you wonder, you cogitate behind your level and perceptive gaze, I find he makes me stutter, as if my head were suddenly a void! Does he do this to you, unbrain you, my skull is like — well, what — an old woman's room, does he do this to you?
SECOND MOTHER: Never —
EMPRESS: Well, you are lucky in all ways... (*Pause. No sound but from the street below.*) Can you explain to me what sexual preference is? (*Pause*)
Its arbitrary — (*Pause*)

Its pitiless arbitrariness — (*Pause*)
Its — (*Pause*)
Well, I longed to see you. I had to see you. And I have!
(*To the* SERVANT.)
Tell the coach, get lost, I walk home unattended and may take hours. (*The* SERVANT *leaves. To* STARHEMBERG.) You must talk more. You force the most undigested vomit of dissonance and trash from those surrounding you, which is a gambit on your part, like everything, I believe nothing you do is not calculated in utter coldness, and you let your mother stink. (*She turns, stops.*) They want to name a regiment the Starhemberg but someone must present the colours. Do it. In the knowledge they will splash their flesh against some wall in Hungary. (*He bows.*) The Turks chop off their genitals, why is that? And the noses, why is that?

STARHEMBERG: They are afraid to love.

EMPRESS: Aren't we? (*To* SECOND MOTHER.) I was so curious to meet you. And of course, it all makes sense. (*She turns to leave.*)

SECOND MOTHER: He came up behind me, on a hill.

EMPRESS: Who did?

SECOND MOTHER: And he — so wanted to touch me — such suffering — it marked me — like a disfigurement — I could not turn but felt his awful stare — I felt my entire body flush with blood — the kidneys gush — the whole length of my bowel — hot rush of blood —

EMPRESS: That is a poem — (*Pause. She looks at* STARHEMBERG.) She did not think that. It is a poem. By Ady. **Absurd**! I know the poem by heart. (*She goes out.*)

Scene 7

A park in Vienna. KATRIN *sits for the* PAINTER. SUSANNAH *watches.*

SUSANNAH: My throbbing priest. My cogent and distended priest I **love him terribly and all he does is write me notes**. (*Pause*) He is addicted to these little notes which are surely — which are half-hearted penetrations, surely? I don't understand a word of them, I hold them this way up, and that way up, I read them diagonally, I cut them up with scissors, scatter them and pick them up again I **have struck him twice across the jaw** and do you blame me? And oh, he was white! White with pride and reticence and then forgave me. He wanted to hit me but he didn't, he forgave me instead. What is all this **didn't** with him? I want a child. God knows why. What do I want a child for?

KATRIN (*maintaining her pose*): It is not a matter of you wanting a child. It is the child wanting. I know. I never wanted a child. But the child wanted. All this 'I never asked to be born' etcetera, piss and nonsense! I know. The unborn, the unconceived, force the act upon the parents **Get her on the ground it says. Get him in your body it says.** I know. I do know all this. You must get knowledge, Susannah, from anywhere, but get it.

SUSANNAH: Knowledge?

KATRIN: Yes, and make yourself again! There, now I've given you all this time, and all the time I've given you is time lost for myself, what am I, a charity? (*She holds her belly.*) It moves, my master... (*Pause*) Do feel him... he is every bit as violent as his fathers... (SUSANNAH *touches her belly.*) He is perfectly loathesome the way he shoves. He longs to be out and about and intent on damage! **He rampages!** (SUSANNAH *withdraws.*) Pity the land when he is out. Do you think I will be proud of him, and secretly gloat at every little crime he does? Mums do, they worship their terrors, their stabbings they collect like exam certificates. I know. I dread the criminality of motherhood. It is a criminal relation.

PAINTER: From here on a good day you can see to Transylvania... (*He peers, holding his brush.*)

KATRIN (*inspired*): Imagine a room, crowded, locked and barred, in which a poison cloud has drifted...! Imagine the mother of the infant trampling the occupants, her heels, her spikes, go into eyes and cheeks as she climbs the dying mound for the last cubic inch of oxygen, the infant stretched aloft, **spare mine**! Oh, I have blinded you with my heel, oh, I have punctured your face, **spare mine**! (*She smiles.*) Accurate. Oh, so accurate... (*She closes her eyes.*)

SUSANNAH (*to* PAINTER): You're a man. You're a man, aren't you? Why should a man not wish to make love?

PAINTER (*staring, off*): Europe, how it shines! As if a grimy sheet were lifted off, and sunlight fell on all its fields and forests!

KATRIN: And its graves. Its wonderful acres of graves!

SUSANNAH: Is it to torture me? As for fidelity, he asks for none, which makes it worse. **I want to be forced to be faithful**.

PAINTER: The war, how tedious it was! I ached to paint women.

KATRIN: Women are in wars. Where were you?

SUSANNAH: And his thing is hard against me. A branch of maleness. So it is not impotence, surely?

PAINTER: I do so adore the company of women...!

SUSANNAH: He had me once, of course. But that was prostitution. That was opportunism. That was not love, or if it was love, love of a different — (*She stops, following his distracted gaze.*) What are you looking at? I am short-sighted, what?

PAINTER (*putting aside his brush, taking up his sketchbook as if by habit*): They are executing a man... (*He drifts away, drawn inexorably to the scene.*)

KATRIN: Who? Who! (*She prepares to follow him.*) I must watch.

SUSANNAH: Why?

KATRIN: I must, that's all. (*She drifts a little way.*) It's a park. This is a park, and they — (*She goes out.* SUSANNAH, *alone, goes to the canvas. Slowly. Her body is convulsed by shuddering. She grasps the easel for support, embracing it. The front of her dress is smothered in paint. She recovers.* KATRIN *returns.*)

KATRIN: The head fell... no... it did not fall... it spun... it whirled away like a top... and the blood was four fountains... four geysers... but... obviously, he could still see... the head could see as it flew and he knew... he both knew himself to be decapitated and also registered the crazy nature of his flight... his confusion... and his... clarity...! (*She sees* SUSANNAH's *dress.*) You have ruined your dress... (*The* PAINTER *appears with a head.*)

PAINTER: The consciousness is draining out of him... (SUSANNAH *turns away.*)

KATRIN: He can still see...

PAINTER: Yes... he sees us... as through a telescope reversed...

KATRIN: Down tunnels which are darkening...

PAINTER: Our hostile stares are —

KATRIN: Not hostile —

PAINTER: Our curious stares...

KATRIN: Peer down from daylight, as if into a darkening cell... (*The* PAINTER *puts the head on the grass and begins sketching.*)

PAINTER: Unfortunately he lopped his tartar hair, the better to conceal himself —

KATRIN: Absurd!

PAINTER: Absurd, with eyes like those —

KATRIN: Which proclaim his distant origins... (*He sketches feverishly.*)

PAINTER: He was captured in an alley.

KATRIN (*plucking flowers*): The alley is the European thing the silly horseman could not hope to navigate. Oh, silly horseman, I do feel such contempt for him...! (*She drapes the flowers round the head.*)

SUSANNAH: Do stop it...

KATRIN: Stop it, why?

SUSANNAH: **Stop it, I said**. (*The* PAINTER *looks up, sees her dress, then the canvas.*)

PAINTER: Oh, bloody God, you've — (*He throws down his pencil as* TWO EXECUTIONERS *enter, one with a sword, the other lumbering a crucifix.*)

SHYBAL: I can't let you keep the head.

KATRIN: That's all right, we don't want the head.

SHYBAL: Which is peculiar, when the country is so head-choked...

KATRIN (*handing it to him*): Oh, but rules are rules...

McNOY (*popping the head in a sack*): He was not bad, Johnny the Turk...

KATRIN: Oh, really, wasn't he?

McNOY: The women liked him.

KATRIN: Did they? Peculiar, the female nature. Deep as a pool. Or shallow as a puddle, arguably. What do you say?
McNOY: We're country boys.
KATRIN: No, female nature, though?
McNOY: Yokels, I say...
KATRIN: **Don't say yokels** why did they like him **yokels my arse** do say what it is with women that they do so swiftly turn themselves upside down for strangers —
SUSANNAH: Katrin —
KATRIN: **Country boys** no, they do so lurk inside their ignorance, they do so skulk inside their illiteracy as if it were a cave **like Turks why did they like them say.** (*Pause.* SHYBAL *stares at her.*)
SHYBAL: I found it in a Turkish trench, this crucifix. They had chopped bits off it, and it bled.
McNOY: And wept. It does at times, still bleed and weep... (KATRIN *looks at it.*)
KATRIN: Yes, I can see it does...
SHYBAL: And now we carry it, down all the lines, gun on left shoulder, Christ on right!
KATRIN: Yes... good... **Love Christ and wreck his enemies!**
SHYBAL (*looking into her*): I think you were one of them.
KATRIN: What?
SHYBAL: Turks' woman... (*They go off, passing* STARHEMBERG. *She turns to him, sudden and brittle.*)
KATRIN: We only meet in public places! Is that because you follow me? Or do you feel you can be more familiar in a park? Why not? What's a park, in any case, a rather dirty place **blood on the grass.** (*Pause*) Starhemberg, I am frightened of everyone, especially you, and I would not be otherwise, I am so alive with fear, I am skinless, I am flayed and the nerves tremble on the slightest passage of a man like leaves on birches flutter at the poorest breeze...
STARHEMBERG: I feel them.
KATRIN: Good. To fear is to be alive. Of course I shan't live to be old, the body cannot take the strain.
STARHEMBERG: I dog you.
KATRIN: Yes, you do, and I find your face terrible. You know you have a terrible face **don't touch me** I would shudder if you touched me and some cry would issue from the very bottom of my gut like afterbirth sings in the grate or a green log screams, no, I wish to marry a young man of no character whose good looks charm my mother and whose manners are immaculate, a lover of families who will spend all Christmas round the fire, perhaps a teacher at the university when they open it again, and so ambitious, **so very ambitious!** He will know how to demolish any argument, his humour will be infectious and —
STARHEMBERG: You have no mother.
KATRIN: So what —
STARHEMBERG: Your mother perished the same day as you.

KATRIN: I did not perish —
STARHEMBERG: Yes.
KATRIN: You see, he must know everything, **how did I perish I was made**. (*Pause*) Let us leave the park — Susannah — (*She extends a hand to her.*) The park fills me with despair — Susannah — hardly have the howitzers ceased and the prams are out — look, they are pulling a gun out of its pit and the nanny rushes in to spread the picnic cloth, **the speed of oblivion!** (*She shudders, her hand still stretched.*) All right, kiss me if it helps you, press your thin mouth to my thin mouth, all cracked with wind... (*He does not move.* SUSANNAH *gets up, takes her hand.*) How well am I known? Is it selling, my print? (*They start to go.*)
STARHEMBERG: Help me, or I think we'll die alone...
KATRIN: Why not? Why not die alone? How would you die? To the sound of violins, with your children clinging to your feet as if your soul could be pulled back through the ceiling? **Help you how.** (*Pause, she looks at him, laughs, then the women go out.* STARHEMBERG *is left alone on a darkening stage, which fills with members of the Academy, clapping the entrance of* LEOPOLD.)

Scene 8

A circle of CRITICS *at The Imperial Academy of Art.* LEOPOLD *enters to polite applause.*

LEOPOLD: Not the room as we would want it. Not the salon we would choose, the swags being somewhat chipped and the putti lacking gilt, but in such pock-marked landscapes imagination might erupt, I call upon you to elucidate the principles of a new art, because the stir of Europe from its sleep commands a terrible and unrelenting movement of the soul. I only have half an hour. What shall the art be like now, you say! (*He sits. Pause.*) Yes, you say. (*Pause*)
ARST: A People's Art.
LEOPOLD: No. Anybody else? (ARST *sits. Another rises.*)
FELIKS: An art of celebration.
LEOPOLD: What do you want to celebrate?
FELIKS: Us, of course!
LEOPOLD: You? What is there to celebrate in you? The fact you are alive and not a stinking thing among the pine trees? Well, you go and celebrate that, but don't ask us to join you.
STENSH: A celebration of the heroism of the —
LEOPOLD: No, no, leave out the heroism, please, the heroism was not conspicuous, in my own case barely perceptible, and much as

we have reason to be grateful to the Polish cavalry I think an art based on lancers is likely to become repetitive, debased, mechanical, and pleading muslims just as bad, we must move on, **celebrate what exactly**, Bomberg, you speak, your dark face is full of irritation, which is inspiration, surely? (*Pause.* BOMBERG *does not rise.*)

BOMBERG: Shame. An art of shame.

LEOPOLD: Elucidate.

BOMBERG: That's all.

ARST: What is there to be ashamed of? (BOMBERG *shakes his head.*) No, don't just shake your head, that is appalling arrogance... (*He shakes it again.*) I think that gesture is typical of Professor Bomberg, who is needless to say, not among the most popular of teachers —

LEOPOLD: **Who cares if he is popular**? (*Pause* ARST *concedes with a movement of the shoulders.*)

ARST: The fact is the students are unwilling even to attend his lectures which —

LEOPOLD: **Who cares about the students**?

ARST: Well —

LEOPOLD: **Everything you say is meaningless**. (*Pause*) All that matters is whether he is right. (*Pause*) On the other hand, Bomberg, do speak. (*Pause*)

BOMBERG: First, we must know who we are. And to know who we are, we must know who we were. I do not think at this moment, we know who we were, and consequently —

FELIKS: You will depress the people with your introspection.

ARST: He knows nothing of the people, go into the street and see the people, you talk to nobody —

FELIKS: Listen to the people —

BOMBERG: The people have a million mouths —

ARST: You see, you are a pessimist —

BOMBERG: **You want to claim the people. You want to own the people. None of you trusts the people**.

ARST: This is why his lectures are so ill-attended —

BOMBERG: **You suffocate the people —**

LEOPOLD: Bomberg —

BOMBERG: **You invent the people —**

LEOPOLD: Bomberg —

BOMBERG: Shut up about the people! (*Pause*)

ARST: The people clamour for solidarity —

BOMBERG: No, they ache for truth —

FELIKS: Happiness, surely —

BOMBERG: Fuck happiness —

FELIKS: You see? What's wrong with happiness?

LEOPOLD: **Bring in a happy painter! You!** (*He points out the* PAINTER.) Stand up. Don't be intimidated by men with words, you can pick words out of the gutter.

ARST: It is where the best words are.

LEOPOLD: Rubbish. Rubbish and condescension. (ARST *shrugs bitterly.*) Shh! (*To the* PAINTER.) Are you a happy person?
ARST: This is not exactly what we had in mind —
LEOPOLD: Shh! You want to dominate everything! These also are the people. These are the ones whom we must trust. (ARST *shrugs again.*) **I wish you would not shrug like that.** (*To the* PAINTER.) Are you happy?
PAINTER: I — (*Pause*) No.
LEOPOLD: Why not?
PAINTER: I — perhaps a defect in my character —
BOMBERG: **It's not a defect it's a quality.**
LEOPOLD: Shh! If only — may I say this and then forget it — how I wish you gentlemen had shown such viciousness when Islam thrust its bayonets between the city gates — if only — now forget it! (*To the* PAINTER.) Can you paint happy pictures? And if not, why not?
PAINTER: It is not a happy time.
ARST: Then why not make it so?
FELIKS: I think that's asking a great deal of —
ARST: Is it? Why? He is a craftsman, isn't he, he has a duty to the people — (BOMBERG *lets out a long and terrible cry.*) yes — yes— a duty to — God lent him the skill and — what he does with it is — yes —
LEOPOLD: Who do you love?
PAINTER: Who do I love?
LEOPOLD: Not woman. Artist. Which?
PAINTER: Giovanni Carpeta.
FELIKS: Be serious.
PAINTER: Giovanni Carpeta.
ARST: Miserable, satanic, gloom-sodden egoist of idiotically unreal landscapes which —
PAINTER: I don't agree —
ARST: Which induce suicidal thoughts in those already suicidal —
PAINTER: Nevertheless —
ARST: And sends you lurching for the sunlight — one looks at Carpeta and sees at once why the young are turning in their droves to the Spanish and Chinese Schools —
BOMBERG: So what —
ARST: What does Carpeta say, what does Carpeta lend to people already crippled with despair —
PAINTER: He speaks to me —
ARST: I don't think a single canvas of the man would last two minutes in the market square —
PAINTER: **I revere him! I revere him!**
ARST: It would be torn from its stretcher and the crowd would say —
PAINTER: **I revere him!**
ARST: You insult us with your pessimism — (*The* PAINTER *lets*

out a long moan.) Yes, your human loathing — end of speech! (*He shows empty hands. The* PAINTER *sobs.*)

LEOPOLD (*to* the PAINTER): You have to — I'm afraid — defend your soul against the bullies of the mind...

ARST: I must say I am extremely weary with souls, which as far as I can see are merely pretexts for self-adulation.

PAINTER (*to* ARST): I must tell you... if I meet you again, I'll kill you...

ARST: **Now who's the bully**! (*He laughs. The* PAINTER *leaves.*) Soul, I assume? The passing of soul? (*Pause, then to* ARST's *horror*, BOMBERG *grips him from behind about the throat.* LEOPOLD *bursts out laughing.* FELIKS *tries to unlock* BOMBERG's *manic grip. The* EMPRESS *appears.*)

LEOPOLD: **I laugh! I laugh!**

ARST (*as* BOMBERG *releases him, falling back into his chair*): Mad — man...!

LEOPOLD: Bomberg, I think you must join the church... (BOMBERG *shakes his head, weeping into his hands.*) Yes, he must take Orders, mustn't he?

FELIKS: This has been a foolish meeting —

STARHEMBERG: It is a very foolish time. The snake cut into seven pieces writhes absurdly as it tries to join itself, but in what order! How could it otherwise...?

LEOPOLD: You speak. You've said nothing yet.

STARHEMBERG: Nothing I say will be true.

EMPRESS: We don't ask for miracles.

STARHEMBERG: Everything I say I will later retract.

LEOPOLD: We are familiar with this tendency.

STARHEMBERG: The apparent logic of my position is only the dressing of flagrant incompatibilities.

EMPRESS: Obviously, And that is why we trust you, Starhemberg. (*Pause*)

STARHEMBERG: What I need. And what there will be. I need an art which will recall pain. The art that will be will be all flourishes and celebration. I need an art that will plummet through the floor of consciousness and free the unborn self. The art that will be will be extravagant and dazzling. I need an art that will shatter the mirror in which we pose. The art that will be will be all mirrors. I want to make a new man and new woman but only from the pieces of the old. The new man and new woman will insist on their utter novelty. I ask a lot. The new art will ask nothing. And now I am going to bed...

EMPRESS: I do not think, Starhemberg, you have quite grasped the temper of the times, has he? I think what Europe needs is roccocco and a little jazz! (STARHEMBERG *gets up, bows, is about to leave, but stops.*)

STARHEMBERG: During the war, while the ground rose under the shellfire and the sky was black with rising and falling and rising clods, and rising and falling flesh, and everything was racing from itself, the eye from the socket and the arm from the joint, you heard in the fractional silences a singing record going round, deep in a cellar, and the lips of the soon-to-be-dead were mouthing sentiments of banal happiness...

EMPRESS: And why not...? (*He bows, goes out.*) **Why not.** (*The sound of a popular march played by a band, rising to a crescendo.*)

ACT TWO

Scene 1

A bed in a public square, overlooked by benches. STARHEMBERG *watches an* OLD WOMAN *dragging a sheet over the stage. She flings it on the bed.*

STARHEMBERG: Have you given birth?
MIDWIFE: To a proper bastard.
STARHEMBERG: Tell me then, what to expect.
MIDWIFE: Abuse, ducks.
STARHEMBERG: Abuse? Why abuse? It's supposed to be a miracle.
MIDWIFE: So was the saving of Vienna, but all I heard was blasphemy.
STARHEMBERG: Birth's a thing of beauty, surely?
MIDWIFE: It's a thing of pain.
STARHEMBERG: Yes, but pain's divisible.
MIDWIFE: It divided me. I thought I'd never come together again.
STARHEMBERG (*turning away*): Oh, choke on your wit, I'm sorry I bothered you. (ORPHULS *appears*.) **Humour! Humour!** They creep among jokes like the lonely sentry in fortifications! I say pain's divisible. There's pain for something and pain for nothing, so birth's tolerable and torture's sheer disintegration, surely? (*He looks at him*.) I am thinner than yesterday, and you are even fatter.
ORPHULS: No, I am —
STARHEMBERG: Yes, you swell with gratification —
ORPHULS: On the contrary, I am deprived —
STARHEMBERG: Then you swell on that. Everything agrees with you. (*He goes close to him*.) I think all teeth rotted in the siege but yours. **That's her bed**. Where are you sitting? (*He goes to the* WOMAN.) Mother, how much are the benches?
MIDWIFE: I do the bed.
STARHEMBERG: Oh, she is bed specialist. (*He calls off*.) **Bench Man!**
ORPHULS: Is she — has her labour begun?
MIDWIFE: There's been some show, so I get on.
STARHEMBERG: **Bench Man!**
ORPHULS: I think this is — I know you are full of admiration for her but —

STARHEMBERG: The benchman is elsewhere, making humour from his cataracts —

ORPHULS: What is the virtue in it?

STARHEMBERG: Or showing his stumps and making fun of the absent legs —

ORPHULS: I ask you, what —

STARHEMBERG: **No virtue in it. None**. (LEOPOLD *enters.* ORPHULS *sits disconsolately on a bench.*)

LEOPOLD: It's cold, I shan't stay for all of it. And what's her game, in any case? I told Elizabeth this had to be illegal. No, she said, not yet! (*The* AUDIENCE *is drifting in.* LEOPOLD *spots the* PAINTER.) Here is the vantage point! (*He propels the* PAINTER *to the front.*) This also is a battle! And now it rains! She gets all she asks for! (*He pulls up his collar. Umbrellas go up.* KATRIN *appears, supported by the* MIDWIFE. *Silence descends. She looks into the crowd. Pause.*)

KATRIN: Not as many as I'd hoped. Don't they like a spectacle? Not the numbers I'd predicted, but — (*A spasm of pain doubles her. The* MIDWIFE *goes to assist her.* KATRIN *pushes her away.*) **Nobody help me birth the child**. (*Pause. She steadies herself.*) Can everybody see all right? Some people — over there — the view's restricted, surely? (*Pause. She stares into the* AUDIENCE.)

I bring you hope.
I bring you history. (*She is doubled again. The* MIDWIFE *goes to assist but is repelled.*)
What are you —

MIDWIFE: Only helping, lady —

KATRIN: No, that isn't it —

MIDWIFE: Helping —

KATRIN: **That's not what it is**. (*Pause. The* MIDWIFE *looks to* LEOPOLD, *to* ORPHULS.)

MIDWIFE: This is how we get in labour — all abusive, but we don't mean anything —

KATRIN: **I do mean something**.

MIDWIFE: I know darling, but — (*A further spasm. She staggers.*)

LEOPOLD: I can't watch this! (*He half-turns away.*) I can't watch this! Do something, somebody! (ORPHULS *goes to move, with the* MIDWIFE, *but* STARHEMBERG *blocks them, drawing a knife.*)

STARHEMBERG: I'll burst the spleen of anyone who nears her bed. (*A pause.*)

ORPHULS: She is delirious.

STARHEMBERG: She is lucid.

ORPHULS: She is in agony!

STARHEMBERG: Her pain she needs. Her suffering she requires. **No thieving by the compassionate!** (*Pause.* KATRIN *struggles on the bed.*)

LEOPOLD: Starhemberg, if she dies, you are responsible. (*Pause*)

MIDWIFE: You are in such a bad position, lady...!

KATRIN: Good! Let it find daylight through my arse!

MIDWIFE: You see, that's 'ow they go, let me —
STARHEMBERG (*threatening*): Move and you die.
MIDWIFE: **I'm a woman, aren't I?**
ORPHULS: Starhemberg, you are under some awful curse... (*A cry from* KATRIN. *She clutches her belly*.)
LEOPOLD: **End this! I can't watch this!** (MEN, *and the* MIDWIFE, *rush forward, overwhelming* STARHEMBERG, *who is disarmed and held.* KATRIN *is covered with umbrellas.* NUNS *drape the scene of birth. The* EMPRESS *appears*.)
EMPRESS (*going to him, where he is still held*): Starhemberg, was that real love? (*He looks at the ground*.) Not if love's caring, but maybe caring's base?
STARHEMBERG: They pretend to pity her, but they steal her pain. Don't chain her in some madhouse.
EMPRESS: It's you they wish to chain... (*She indicates with a move of her head that* STARHEMBERG *be released. A cry of joy and applause from the birth place*.)
LEOPOLD: It's over, and alive! (A BABY *is handed to* LEOPOLD. *He holds it high*.) What history spoiled, let History mend. I christen her — Concilia! (*Applause. The* CHILD *is handed to a* SERVANT. LEOPOLD *and the* EMPRESS *depart*.)
ORPHULS (*to* STARHEMBERG): Come to Christ, now....
STARHEMBERG: I do. I come to you at all hours. I raise you from your bed and beg you reasons why I should love men.
ORPHULS: Christ also suffered the intensest hate, or He could never have found charity. The good have little purchase on the memory. Who would follow the innocent? No, you follow him who triumphs over himself, who boils within and in whose eyes all struggle rages. Him you follow to the water's edge, and no other... (*He kisses* STARHEMBERG's *hand*.)
KATRIN (*from the bed*): Starhemberg! (STARHEMBERG *turns to go to her.* ORPHULS *clings to his hand*.)
ORPHULS: I must become a bishop.
STARHEMBERG: You must, it's obvious. (*He goes to her*.)
KATRIN: It's perfect, isn't it? Quite perfect?
STARHEMBERG: No loving husband could have made a better child in sheets of wedded honour.
KATRIN: They cheated me...
STARHEMBERG: Yes.
KATRIN: And made of my horrors reconciliation.
STARHEMBERG: Yes.
KATRIN: **History they made of me.**
STARHEMBERG: Yes, but we will deny them yet...
KATRIN (*with a wail*): How...? How...? (*Pause, then* STARHEMBERG *walks away. The* MIDWIFE *accosts him*.)
MIDWIFE: You have some pain, mister...
STARHEMBERG: Pain? Me?

MIDWIFE: I think you will find death difficult.
STARHEMBERG: Yes. I won't have it near me.
MIDWIFE: You tease me, but I'd give you good advice if you would let me.
STARHEMBERG: Do! I like the fact your hands are caked in blood. So were mine until recently. (*The* MIDWIFE *goes close to him, intimately.*)
MIDWIFE: Hang yourself. (*Pause.* STARHEMBERG *nods, as if in appreciation. The* MIDWIFE *squeals with laughter. He seizes her hand. She senses danger.*)
STARHEMBERG: It's you that must hang.
MIDWIFE: Only a joke!
STARHEMBERG: Yes, but I have no sense of humour. (*The* EMPRESS *appears. The* MIDWIFE *hurries away, off.*)
EMPRESS: Starhemberg...
STARHEMBERG: She is a witch, the midwife. She must hang. (*Pause*)
EMPRESS: If you say so.
STARHEMBERG (*calling*): **Don't let her escape, there!**
EMPRESS: Starhemberg, your mother's dead... (*He looks at her.*)
STARHEMBERG: Once they are in the slums, it takes a regiment to find them... (*Pause.* ORPHULS *goes to* STARHEMBERG *and embraces him swiftly.*) Dead? But I hadn't finished with her yet...
ORPHULS: We shall bury her...
STARHEMBERG: I shall have to see her naked, shan't I? I shall have to wash her and she was not clean...
ORPHULS: We'll bury your mother...
STARHEMBERG: Together...
ORPHULS: Yes...
STARHEMBERG: And then, perhaps... kill yours... (*Pause. He departs.* ORPHULS *is left alone as night falls.*)

Scene 2

A plot in the city. ORPHULS *alone.* SUSANNAH *enters.*

SUSANNAH: I would lick you all over if you'd let me. I would take your testicles in my mouth and roll them gently as if they were blown eggs of such rarity, of such fragility. I would take your arse in my hands if you'd let me and raise it like a sacrifice, oh, listen, I must tell you I will marry somewhere else if you don't give me your flesh to love. An officer with four cows has made me a proposal. (*He turns to look at her.*)
ORPHULS: Marry him. (*Pause*)
SUSANNAH: I will. I will marry him.

ORPHULS (*turning away*): And lie awake whole wretched nights with your brain bursting. I will crouch in your imagination like a bear in a crate. I will pace there all your hours.

SUSANNAH: I will have children, whose wailing will drown out your memory.

ORPHULS: It's a tempting prospect, I can see, red-armed on the acre and a basketful of screamers. Is he drunk, this officer? Drunk and poxed? As he climbs on you to satisfy some savagery the cows will bellow in the downstairs room, what perfection! And how far from the city? They say there is rough pasture eighty miles outside Vienna where the old troopers are settling, though the bodies of the Janissaries must be cleared from it, **you cataclysmic bitch**, all you have will disintegrate in a single winter! (*He turns, to* OTHERS *offstage.*) **Here!** (*He points to the earth. Cloaked* FIGURES *enter with shovels.*) And not deep. (*They begin to excavate the spot.*)

SUSANNAH: What have you done...?

WORKMAN: **Here!** (*They dig faster.*)

SUSANNAH: What have you done...!

ORPHULS: I shall inhabit you. I shall swim your veins and smile like a gargoyle from the walls of your womb...

SUSANNAH (*as* LEOPOLD *and* OTHERS *enter*): What has he done! (ORPHULS *laughs as* SUSANNAH *runs off.*)

LEOPOLD: Not funny! Where?

WORKMAN: Here! (*The* EMPRESS *goes to look at the excavation.*)

LEOPOLD: Don't look! (*She persists*) Hideous! Don't look! (*She ignores him.*) All right, look if you must. (LEOPOLD *goes to* ORPHULS.) Are you mad? **Cover the grave!** What is to become of Vienna? You want to be a bishop and you kill your mother, are you mad? **Cover it entirely!** We are building a new Europe and you do this, you are in love with Starhemberg, he eats your soul, you horrify me! (*The* EMPRESS *joins them.*) We must arrest him and declare him mad. What else do you suggest?

ORPHULS: I am not mad. I am perfectly normal, only more so.

LEOPOLD: **In what sense!**

ORPHULS: I was never more fitted for my task.

LEOPOLD: **What task!** (*He turns to the* EMPRESS.) He looks the perfect cleric, he exudes authority, who would not confess to him the most lurid sin and yet — (*He turns to* ORPHULS.) Do you want to be tried, is that what you want? Do you want to be hanged, is that what you want?

ORPHULS: Perhaps.

LEOPOLD: Perhaps? You require it, obviously!

ORPHULS: I require unhappiness, that's obvious.

EMPRESS: And this is such a happy age! There never was such happiness! All this happiness, and you go and bash your mother with a rock. Was it a rock?

ORPHULS: A plank.

EMPRESS: A plank. (LEOPOLD *groans.*)

ORPHULS: She placed no value on her life. It was a burden to her. Whereas her death meant much to me. So all things pointed to her extinction.

LEOPOLD: Especially Starhemberg! His finger, especially. I might have wished to kill my mother. What if I had, what should I have been!

ORPHULS: Excessively alive. (*He holds* LEOPOLD.) It is a second birth, and like the first, induces such a rush of air to unopened lungs, I struggled on the ground red as an infant, my unused limbs thrashing the air, and he carried me, he bore me home like the maternal nurse! There! (*He points.*) There is the site of my nativity! (*Pause*)

LEOPOLD: A new morality we asked for. And we get this.

ORPHULS: Feel me! I'm **new**.

LEOPOLD: Take your claw off me! You should shrivel in a furnace, and the skull, as it popped, should invite spontaneous applause!

EMPRESS: Oh, do be quiet —

LEOPOLD: **You say be quiet and** —

EMPRESS: Think. Think.

LEOPOLD: When I think of my mother —

EMPRESS: That is not thinking, is it? Stop generalising and think. (*She looks at* ORPHULS, *who smiles.*) What have you learned?

ORPHULS: Learned...?

EMPRESS: Learned, yes, for neither you nor Starhemberg do things except for learning. Deliver us your sermon. Not on murder, but what came of it. Quick, now! And you! (*She calls to the* WORKMEN.) Yes! Down your tools and gather, cluster the Bishop, who will speak, cluster him, he knows things you do not. (*She turns away, waiting. The* MEN *reluctantly form a circle.* ORPHULS *prepares, and then with the force of inspiration, turns to deliver his oration.*

ORPHULS: All that occurs, does it not occur that I should be its beneficiary, nourished on it, be it filth or excellence? Even the death of love is food to the soul and therefore what is evil? Is there evil except not to do? I do not blaspheme when I say the gift of life is paltry and our best service to God is not to thank Him, endless thanking, no, but to enhance His offer, and yet you do not, I think if I were God I would declare with some weariness or even vehemence, how little they do with the breath I gave them, they exhale repetitions, they applaud the lie, they sleep even in their waking hours, why did I make them thus, I erred in some respect, they fill me with disgust, have you no notion of God's horror? I am thinking of the God in us whose profound groan is the background to our clatter — (*He identifies one of the uncomprehending* WORKMEN.) You shake your head in silence, is that freedom? If silence was freedom it is so no longer, the word is volatile, am I too difficult for you? **Liar! You hide behind the so-called simplicity of Christ, but is that not a blasphemy?** (*Pause*) If I had not done evil, how could I address you who have perhaps thought evil only? If I did not know cruelty could I know pity, they are the twin towers of the soul? Do not hold hands in false gestures as if by crowding you could exclude the groan of God, no, you must hear the sound of His despair, and we must learn from Judas whose Gospel is not written, we must learn from him who stood alone, for Judas did not sell Christ nor was he corrupt, but Judas was cruel for knowledge, and without Judas there could be no resurrection, Beauty, Cruelty, and Knowledge, these are the triple order of the Groaning God, I speak as your adviser in whose pain you may see beauty, I praise my beauty and you must praise yours! (*Pause*) I end here, in a proper and terrible exhaustion. I have laid myself before you, which is the duty of a priest. (*Pause*)

EMPRESS: How wonderful you are... I shall not forget one word you said. How wonderful you are, I could truly love you. But we can't know that, and you must die... mustn't he? (*She looks at* LEOPOLD. *The bell of a great church.*)

Scene 3

A room in Vienna, shuttered. The bell ceases. Into the obscurity, STARHEMBERG *walks slowly. He removes his clothing, item by item. He goes to a chair, and sits.* KATRIN *is discovered, already naked, in a chair distantly opposite his own. They gaze, unfalteringly.*

KATRIN: I show myself to you. I show myself, and it is an act of love. Stay in your place!

STARHEMBERG: I was not moving. Only looking.

KATRIN: You were not moving, no... (*Pause*) I am in such a torment it would be an act of pity to approach me, pure pity, but you will not, will you? I know because you are not kind, thank God, you spare us kindness, and your body is quite grey, it is so far from perfect, spare us perfection also! You are a beautiful man, so beautiful my breath is stiff as mud to breathe, don't come near me.

STARHEMBERG: You shudder...

KATRIN: Yes, may I call you my love, whether or not you love me I must call you my love, **don't get up!**

STARHEMBERG: I shan't get up...

KATRIN: I am in the most beautiful Hell. Praise me a little, mutter me a bit, describe, describe for Christ in Heaven's sake, I could gnaw your knees to blood, and you mine, I know you could —

STARHEMBERG: Yes...

KATRIN: I would rather take one look from you than pulp a night in hopeless effort, there, I'm better now, much better... (*Pause*) It's odd, but though I have done all that suggested itself to me, I never looked at any man but you, I think. Looked, I mean. I never knew to look was love. (*Pause*)

What do you see?
What do you see? (SUSANNAH *enters, opening the shutters one by one.*)

SUSANNAH: My priest is dead. (*Pause. Light floods in.*)
With all Vienna watching. (STARHEMBERG *and* KATRIN *are still.*)
My priest is dead, and I am marrying a farmer. (*She freezes.*)
Not difficult if you try. (*Pause, then* STARHEMBERG *rises, pulls a long coat over himself. A* CHILD's *cries distantly.*)

STARHEMBERG: We are going to Wallachia.

SUSANNAH: Wallachia? Why?

STARHEMBERG: To inspect the forts.

SUSANNAH: What forts?

STARHEMBERG: Within whose compass New Europe is to breathe. Under whose benign regard the vines may ripen undisturbed, and marriages be blessed with endlessness... (*He leans his head on* SUSANNAH's *shoulder.*)

KATRIN: Yes! Show me the frontier! I will study the trajectory of shells, and arcs, dead grounds and fields of fire, I have Holbein, Durer, Montecucculi in my library! What don't I know of wars! (*She pulls a gown over herself as a* NURSE *enters holding* CONCILIA, *crying and swaddled.* STARHEMBERG *goes to the* NURSE *and takes the* CHILD *in his arms.*)

STARHEMBERG: And Concilia! Concilia, obviously! (*He lifts her in the air. A fortress wall descends. The sound of knocking on a door.*)

Scene 4

The fort in Wallachia. STARHEMBERG *alone, half-dressed.*

STARHEMBERG: Come in! (*An* OFFICER *enters.*)

OFFICER: There is a Turkish regiment two miles off.

STARHEMBERG: Whose?

OFFICER: Jemal Pasha's Lancers.

STARHEMBERG: Show Jemal my standard.

OFFICER: That's done already. We think it most unlikely they will attack a fort.

STARHEMBERG: That's my opinion also. (*The* OFFICER *bows, goes to leave.*) Tell Jemal I have a gift for him. Hostages, safe conduct and the rest of it. (*The* OFFICER *bows and is about to leave when* STARHEMBERG *grabs him violently*.) Talk to me! Talk!

OFFICER: Talk...?

STARHEMBERG: Yes, yes, my gorgeous one, lie down and tell me your life.

OFFICER: Lie down?

STARHEMBERG (*propelling him towards a chair*): There — yes —

OFFICER: But that's your —

STARHEMBERG: My cot, yes, but you have it, you spread, you luxuriate, and off with lovely tunics —

OFFICER: I'm rather cold —

STARHEMBERG (*unbuttoning him*): Forget the cold, and I will come to you as a child to a long-lost relative, I will place my head just — there — forget the cold, the cold is not our enemy —

OFFICER: No, I suppose —

STARHEMBERG: Not in the least our enemy, and tell me in a child-like way, for my infant ears, the beauty of your life... (*He lays his head in the* OFFICER's *lap, and draws his hand to his head*.)

OFFICER: Beauty of it...

STARHEMBERG: Yes, do —

OFFICER: I don't know that it's —

STARHEMBERG: Mmm...

OFFICER: That it's very —

STARHEMBERG: Mmm...

OFFICER: Beautiful — I wouldn't —

STARHEMBERG: No, no, make me adore you —

OFFICER: Well, I —

STARHEMBERG: Go on —

OFFICER: I er — I er —

STARHEMBERG: Mmm...

OFFICER: I was —

STARHEMBERG: Mmmm...?

OFFICER: One of — seven children —

STARHEMBERG: Seven! Really? Seven?

OFFICER: And er — was born in Lombardy —

STARHEMBERG: Lombardy?

OFFICER: Yes — land of — er — many poplars there and — I can't remember much of it but —

STARHEMBERG: No, no, paint it! Paint it! Make me love you.

OFFICER: Poplars and — and —

STARHEMBERG: Say, do say... (*The* OFFICER *dries, holds his head in despair*.) Must. Must. (*The* OFFICER *is in agony*.) Must.

OFFICER (*with sudden invention*): I got up one morning — before anybody else — I don't know why — got up and crept downstairs — the sun was brilliant and —

STARHEMBERG: Mmm...

OFFICER: Walked down the street — it's not true, this — the streets were full of — were full of — horses!

STARHEMBERG: Mmmm...

OFFICER: A cavalry brigade were tethered there and — I took one and unbridled it — and rode it — clattering across a bridge — the water was all — chopped and sparkling with sunlight — I rode and rode — up four hills and down four valleys — and when the horse stopped, so did I and I — slid off and —

STARHEMBERG: Yes —

OFFICER: And —

STARHEMBERG: Don't stop! Don't stop!

OFFICER: I saw — a — beautiful girl —

STARHEMBERG: Make it an old man.

OFFICER: What?

STARHEMBERG: An old man. Make it an old man, please.

OFFICER: This old man, and he —

STARHEMBERG: Yes —

OFFICER: He — er — (KATRIN *enters, silently. He observes her. She perches, silently, on a chair.*) He — er — had a long beard — and —

STARHEMBERG: How long?

OFFICER: **Ridiculously long!**

STARHEMBERG: Are you sure?

OFFICER: Yes!

STARHEMBERG: Go on...

OFFICER: Which reached to the ground — and he took my hand — and his hand was — bleeding —

STARHEMBERG: Why?

OFFICER: I don't know why — it was anyway and — I put my little hand in his wet hand —

STARHEMBERG: Why though?

OFFICER: **Don't interrupt!** And led me — willingly — I did not protest to a — a — (*His eyes meet* KATRIN's. *He perseveres.*) well — which when I looked was —

STARHEMBERG: What was in the well?

OFFICER: I'm coming to that —

STARHEMBERG: Forgive me, I —

OFFICER: Was — absolutely —

STARHEMBERG: Yes? Yes?

OFFICER: **Full of bricks!**

STARHEMBERG: Bricks?

OFFICER: Full of bricks, why not bricks!

STARHEMBERG: No reason, I —

OFFICER: Bricks, yes —

STARHEMBERG: That was why his hands were bleeding!

OFFICER: Obviously!
STARHEMBERG: I do like you! I like you very much!
OFFICER: And these bricks were so deep and so jumbled — so chaotic and so — arid —
STARHEMBERG: Yes —
OFFICER: They had caused the death of many animals... (*Pause*) whose bodies... lay littered round the rim... (*Pause*)
STARHEMBERG: They couldn't reach the —
OFFICER: Not a drip... (*Pause. He holds* STARHEMBERG's *hand.*)
STARHEMBERG: Go on...
OFFICER: And the old man begged me — No, he didn't beg me, actually, he — Insisted — Most cruelly insisted that I — unblock the well... And I was only ten...
STARHEMBERG: Ten...
OFFICER: And the sun beat down, and the smell of decomposing sheep was...
STARHEMBERG: Poor boy...
OFFICER: **Vile** and — I thought — Climbing in all that rubble thought — Shifting the bricks, thought...
STARHEMBERG: What?
OFFICER: Many things, but — he was so severe — his ugly face over the rim was going — **Faster! Faster!**
STARHEMBERG: Vile man —
OFFICER: Vile man, yes —
STARHEMBERG: Thirsty, too!
OFFICER: Yes, that must have been — partly the explanation for his vileness, but — I felt — his beard hung over — hideous beard hanging right over — and I —
STARHEMBERG: Yes —
OFFICER: Instead of just throwing the bricks out I —
STARHEMBERG: **You didn't —**
OFFICER: Yes —
STARHEMBERG: **You hit him with the brick**. (*Long pause.*) A terrible, terrible, story... (*Pause. The* OFFICER *gets up, does up his tunic.*)
OFFICER: If I am to reach Jemal, I ought to... was that all right?
STARHEMBERG: So you never drank?
OFFICER: What?
STARHEMBERG: You never drank...
OFFICER: I... no, I suppose not... no... (*He goes out.* STARHEMBERG *dresses in fresh clothes.*)
STARHEMBERG: Bring Concilia... Bring the child of impeccable origins...
KATRIN: It's late.
STARHEMBERG: Yes. Bring her from her little bed.
KATRIN (*puzzled*): Why...?
STARHEMBERG: Concilia, whose forehead is a little swamp of

Imperial kisses, and whose ears are tiny basins of kind sentiment... bring her here...

KATRIN: Why, Starhemberg?

STARHEMBERG (*finishing his dress*): Because we must love each other, now. (KATRIN *looks at him.*) I don't think she has ever seen the stars! (KATRIN *goes out. A cry is heard on the fortifications, which is repeated nearer.*)

THE WATCH: One bo — dy! One bo — dy! (*Pause, then a* TURKISH OFFICER *enters, and stands.*)

STARHEMBERG: Why have your attacks all fallen off? You are good at rushing things but bad at standing under fire. Is that the personality of Turks, or the poor quality of officers? (*Pause*) And always you maim. Coolly, maim. This sickened me for some years, because I thought a cruel act done in temper has its own excuse, but this slow hacking has not even the decent motive of a butcher.

JEMAL: The ceaseless propoganda of the Christian church has stirred up subject races, some of whom we have convincing proof are cutting off parts of their bodies to discredit the Ottoman authorities.

STARHEMBERG: I think it is to do with fear of love. I think in the very moment of the cruellest torture, the perpitrator suffocates the possibility of freedom in himself. And thus is becomes habitual, a narcotic.

JEMAL: You persist in identifying me with all atrocity which is —

STARHEMBERG: No, no, I was merely being philosophical... (KATRIN *enters, holding the* CHILD *in a shawl. She stops, horrified.* STARHEMBERG *looks at her.*) Oh, the great chaos of this continent. The beating of lives in the bowl of obscure quarrels, the batter of perpetual and necessary horror. Who would not be a European if he could? I have a present for Jemal. (*Pause*)

KATRIN: Starhemberg... (*Pause*)

STARHEMBERG: Yes. (*Pause*)

KATRIN: She wants to stay in Austria! (JEMAL *looks at* STARHEMBERG, *confused.*)

STARHEMBERG: Yes, but what has that to do with anything?

KATRIN: She loves us and —

SUSANNAH (*entering*): Shh... (KATRIN *looks with bewilderment, first at* SUSANNAH, *then at* STARHEMBERG.)

KATRIN: I refuse whatever you are —

SUSANNAH: Shh... (*Pause, then suddenly* KATRIN *attempts to leave with the* CHILD, *but* STARHEMBERG *blocks her, holding her firmly. She is still.*)

KATRIN: Love? Did I say love?

JEMAL: This is a most unpleasant thing to witness in a State called civilized and I —

STARHEMBERG: The child's a Turk. (*Pause*)

JEMAL: A Turk?

STARHEMBERG: Of Turkish fathers whose untimely executions left her stranded in this foreign territory... (KATRIN *shudders.*

STARHEMBERG *holds her closer.*) How do we escape from History? We reproduce its mayhem in our lives...

JEMAL: I refuse your gift!

STARHEMBERG: Refuse and you die. And my hostage officer, him too. (STARHEMBERG *takes the* CHILD *from* KATRIN, *who is as if petrified. Suddenly she is seized by a physical delirium.* SUSANNAH *embraces her, overcomes her, stills her. She emerges, smiling, from the ordeal.*)

KATRIN: In any case, she might so easily have been seized in a raid.

STARHEMBERG (*giving the* CHILD *to* JEMAL, *who hesitates*): It happens all the time... (*He holds the baby out.*) You will convert her to the true faith, obviously...

KATRIN: And who knows what might have befallen her if she stayed in Vienna? Smallpox? Carriage accidents? Anything! (JEMAL *takes the* CHILD.) And in a year, it will be as if I never knew her! (*She looks at* JEMAL. *He returns her look, then turns on his heel and goes out. The cry of the* SENTRIES *is heard.*)

THE WATCH: One bo — dy and a child! One bo — dy and a child!

KATRIN (*to* STARHEMBERG): Look at me. What do you see? (*He gazes at her. Suddenly, an eruption of fireworks, explosions and coloured lights, cheering from the entire fort. The* EMPRESS *enters with the court, in riding cloaks.*)

EMPRESS: Starhemberg, who never answers the Imperial Despatch! Starhemberg, obscure in Wallachia! But we will not be deprived! (*She embraces him.* LEOPOLD *enters.*)

LEOPOLD (*greeting* KATRIN): The Mother! And the Child! Where is the child? (*He looks from* KATRIN *to* SUSANNAH.) Concilia, where's she? (*A burst of fireworks.*)

SUSANNAH: She's been returned.

LEOPOLD: Returned?

KATRIN: To her creators. She's with them. (*The* EMPRESS *looks from* KATRIN *to* STARHEMBERG.)

EMPRESS: Starhemberg —

KATRIN: He —

EMPRESS: Starhemberg...?

KATRIN: Wait! (*A firework trickles down the sky.*) Let me finish it. (*she speaks with infinite calculation.*) He has — made — restitution — of — their property — (*Pause*) for which — I — merely was — (*Pause. She grins.*) Curator... (*She grips* LEOPOLD *by the arm. He is horrified.*) Congratulate me!

LEOPOLD: Concilia...!

KATRIN: Congratulate me, then!

LEOPOLD: **Con — cil — ia!**

Con — cil — ia! (*Lights rise and fall.* KATRIN *walks unsteadily to* STARHEMBERG. *They embrace. They kiss.*)

I laugh!

I laugh!

JUDITH
A Parting from the Body

CHARACTERS

JUDITH	A Widow of Israel
HOLOFERNES	A General of Assyria
THE SERVANT	An Ideologist

The tent of a general. HOLOFERNES *alone.*

HOLOFERNES: Tonight I must talk about death. For example, its arbitrary selections. This I find impossible to assimilate. This I find agony to contemplate. Its fingering of one. Its indifference to another. Its beckoning to one. Its blindness to another. This haunts me, this casualness. This gnaws my curiosity. I might say this quality in death has governed my emotions and made battle precious. Come in. For while victory is the object of the battle, death is its subject, and the melancholy of the soldiers is the peculiar silence of a profound love. Do come in, I detest the way some hover round the door, do you think I am deaf? This certainly lends me a quality which some describe as tenderness. Because I walk among the dead they will ascribe to me feelings of shame or of compassion. This is not the case. Rather, I am overcome with wonder. I am trembling with a terrible infatuation. Come in, I said. (JUDITH *enters, kneels, is still.*) This sensitivity they find hard to reconcile with cruelty, for which I also have a reputation. But cruelty is collaboration in chaos, of which the soldiers are merely the agents. It is not without philosophy. And some generals talk of necessity. They talk of limited objectives. There are no limitations, nor is there necessity. There is only infatuation. I hate to be bothered when I am thinking about death. Come in! (*A* SERVANT WOMAN *enters, kneels.*) What a racket even bare feet make for the contemplative mind. Tomorrow the dead will clog the ditches, so I must think. It is perfectly natural to think, however little thought affects the outcome. (*Pause.* JUDITH *produces a bottle. She uncorks it, with a characteristic sound. Pause.*) I do not drink, which if you were not a stranger, you would know. Obviously you believe in rumours, for example, the rumour that cruel men are degenerate. The opposite is the case, I promise you. (*A long pause.*)

THE SERVANT: I heard — futile now, I see — I heard — you liked women. (*She looks at* JUDITH.) Don't you like women either?

HOLOFERNES: Tonight I must talk about death.

THE SERVANT: She talks about death! (*She looks* at JUDITH.) Don't you? All the time she does. Death this, death that. I say to her, you melancholy thing, I don't know what made you like it. No, she is utterly morbid. Aren't you? (*Pause.* JUDITH *stares at the ground.*)

HOLOFERNES: I think you are a poor liar, and she is shallow. I think you have brought me a bitch as a present, a thing that giggles. On some nights I should certainly not cavil, but tonight is different. Tonight —

THE SERVANT: You want to talk about death! Of course you do, and she can, can't you, she's shy, that's all, I promise you on this particular subject she can spout for hours, can't you, go on, show the gentleman how much you. Go on. How well you. Judith. Show him. (*Pause. Suddenly* HOLOFERNES *seizes* the SERVANT, *fixing her tightly in an upright posture, between life and death. Pause.*)

HOLOFERNES: Those who die tomorrow, let us think of them.

THE SERVANT: Yes —

HOLOFERNES: The speed of their final thoughts, the torrent of their last reflections —

THE SERVANT: Yes —

HOLOFERNES: We fight on false presumptions, the first of these being that death will pass us by, I mean the wilful suspension of all logic is what permits the battle, though the battle is itself quite logical —

THE SERVANT: Yes —

HOLOFERNES: We ache for the pain of our companions, I am certain of it, soldiers nourish the secret hope their friends will die, does that horrify you, I only — (*the* SERVANT *chokes*) — seek the truth of battle, does that horrify you, I only probe the ecstasies of pain —

JUDITH: You are killing my property. (HOLOFERNES *is still, rigid.*) My property can't breathe. (*Pause*)

HOLOFERNES: I do not wish to fuck tonight.

JUDITH: No. You wish to talk.

HOLOFERNES: And anyway, this area is out of bounds, didn't you know, it is forbidden to civilians.

JUDITH: Yes.

HOLOFERNES: There are notices everywhere, or can't you read? What possible use are you to me if you can't read, tonight of all nights, when I must argue death, what use is the company of the illiterate?

JUDITH: I could be illiterate and still —

HOLOFERNES: Converse?

JUDITH: I might —

HOLOFERNES: There is no wisdom in the illiterate, I assure you, none —

JUDITH: Oh, I don't know —

HOLOFERNES: No, listen, don't repeat untruths which are merely sentimental —

JUDITH: I wasn't being sentimental, only —

HOLOFERNES: It is a fallacy that ignorance can harbour truth, and you are **so unwelcome**, take this away! (*He releases the* SERVANT, *who slides onto her knees.* JUDITH *does not move. The* SERVANT *breathes deeply in the silence.*) I do like women, but for all the wrong reasons. And as for them, they rapidly see through me. They see I only hide in them, which is not love. They see I shelter in their flesh. Which is not love. Now, go away. (*Pause*)

JUDITH: Let me speak. I cannot promise anything I say will be original. But I'm not unread. And if I say things which don't accord with your experience, it may serve to sharpen your own perceptions. No one can always engage with his equals, sometimes it's beneficial to hear an unsophisticated point of view. And anyway, how do you know you have an equal?

HOLOFERNES: I have no equal in the field I've made my speciality.

JUDITH: Which field is that? Murder or philosophy? (*She is suddenly pained at her cleverness.*)

No, that was —
Give me another chance to —
That was —

HOLOFERNES, *as if oblivious to her, sits in a canvas chair, looking away, as if in thought. In the silence, the cry of a* SENTRY *in the night.*

HOLOFERNES: It is of great importance that the enemy is defeated.

JUDITH: Oh, yes!

HOLOFERNES: Or is it? Perhaps it only seems so.

JUDITH: Seems so?

HOLOFERNES: Always the night before the soldiers die I think — perhaps this is not important, after all. Perhaps it would be better if the enemy defeated us. I mean, from a universal point of view. Perhaps my own view is too narrow.

JUDITH (*thoughtfully*): Yes...

HOLOFERNES: Fortunately this consideration only occurs to me after I have made the plan of battle, never before. It is as if the thought were released by the certain knowledge I shall win.

JUDITH: Yes, but is it certain?

HOLOFERNES: Yes. No matter what the preparations of the enemy we shall win. For one thing, they believe we shall win, which alone ensures that they will lose. Take your clothes off now. As for this gnawing sense I have described that victory lacks authenticity, this disappears with the sunrise.

JUDITH: Take my clothes off... ?

HOLOFERNES: I think it is the persistence and proximity of Death, who lurks in all the interstices of life and cannot be abolished, which justifies the military profession. I think it is abhorrent only to those who lack the intellectual courage to recognise it for what it is — the organization of a metaphor. Did you not want to take your clothes off? What else did you come for? Hang them on a chair. I long to be married, but to a cruel woman. And as I lay dying of sickness in a room, I would want her to ignore me. I would want her to laugh in the kitchen with a lover as my mouth grew dry. I would want her to count my money as I choked.

JUDITH (*in confusion*): I cannot. (*She shakes her head.*) I cannot — simply —

HOLOFERNES: No.

JUDITH: As if —

HOLOFERNES: No.

JUDITH: If you would —

HOLOFERNES: Yes?
JUDITH: Just — touch — or —
HOLOFERNES: Touch?
JUDITH: Or —
HOLOFERNES: Murmur?
JUDITH: Something — just —
HOLOFERNES: I can see how difficult it is for you. Unfortunately I only wish to talk about death. It is you who came to be naked.
JUDITH: Yes, but — naked lovingly.
HOLOFERNES: Lovingly naked?
JUDITH: Yes.
HOLOFERNES: Tomorrow many will be naked. And so humiliated in their nakedness. So cruelly naked and smeared with excrement.
JUDITH: **I can't undress with you —**
HOLOFERNES: Their arses, their silly arses show —
JUDITH: **This is so much harder than I thought.**
HOLOFERNES: Yes, and you have hardly begun. (*Pause. She glares at him. She controls her panic. She turns to the* SERVANT.)
JUDITH: Take my clothing.
THE SERVANT (*smiling*): I've done this before. For Judith. And not only Judith!
JUDITH: He wants me naked. So.
THE SERVANT: All sorts of girls.
JUDITH (*undressing*): Naked I must be.
THE SERVANT (*taking a garment and laying it over her arm*): Some could and some couldn't.
JUDITH: Naked and unashamed.
THE SERVANT: Because undressing is an art.
JUDITH: As if I were not the object of his gaze, but simply the object of my own...
THE SERVANT: Properly done, it's most effective —
JUDITH: As if I were before the mirror and not before — (*She freezes.*) **I can't.** (*Pause*)
THE SERVANT: You've done it before.
JUDITH: Still, I can't.
THE SERVANT: Why ever not? Silly! (*Pause. The* SERVANT *looks to* HOLOFERNES.) She can't... I'm sorry... she is very sensitive... Idiot! No, she is though. She is magnificent but. (*She shakes her head.*) There you are, people are like that, one day flinging it all off and another — it must be you. It must be your. Whatever you have got. That's doing it. I mean. You are a most peculiar man, and I say that with all respect, with every admiration, you throw a girl off her — you would make a prostitute uneasy — and that's not as difficult as you would think, it really isn't, I've known exasperated prostitutes. (*She turns to* JUDITH.) Put this on again, you'll —
JUDITH: No. (*Pause*) I'll stay like this. Half-naked. (*Pause*) I am a widow, I don't know why I mention that. To earn your sympathy, perhaps.

HOLOFERNES: I have no sympathy.
JUDITH: No, I didn't think —
THE SERVANT: Why should he?
JUDITH: I suppose I —
THE SERVANT: He never knew your husband, why should he —
JUDITH (*to the* SERVANT): **Just get out.** (*Pause. The* SERVANT *prepares to go.*)
HOLOFERNES: No. Stay. (*The* SERVANT *looks to* JUDITH.) Wouldn't you prefer to stay? Admit you would prefer that.
JUDITH: Perhaps she would, but I —
HOLOFERNES: No, no, it's me that has to choose, surely? It is my night, not yours. Tomorrow I. Tomorrow they. Flesh on all the hedges. No, it's me, surely? (*Pause. The cry of a* SENTRY *in the night.*) I am a man who never could be loved. I am a man no woman could find pitiful. Pity is love. Pity is passion. The rest is clamour. The rest is just imperative. (*The* SERVANT *looks at* JUDITH. *A silence.*) When I see my soldiers drag a woman in the thorns, her white legs thrashing the air and her squeals oddly harmonious with the squeals of passing transport, I ask myself who is the most pitiful, knowing as I do how sorry for themselves all soldiers are, and how they smother misery among the clods and nettles and disordered clothing of their victims. I find it hard to reprimand them. After all, what is an army? It is the mad life licensed. It is not harmony, is it? It is not harmony on the march. (*Pause*) When a woman loves a man, it is not his manliness she loves, however much she craves it. It is the pity he enables her to feel, by showing, through the slightest aperture, his loneliness. No matter what his brass, no matter what his savage, it creeps, like blood under a door... (*Pause*)
THE SERVANT: It's going to be difficult tonight. I felt as we came in here, it's going to be difficult tonight.
JUDITH: I must admit, Holofernes is not what I expected. I am neither awed nor intimidated, and I can say in perfect honesty, he is not what I expected. It makes things different. It doesn't make them worse. I should dress, in order that — (*She goes to reach for her clothes.*)
HOLOFERNES: No.
JUDITH (*stopping*): I think if we are to engage with one another in —
HOLOFERNES: No.
JUDITH: It is very hard to be — to collect one's thoughts and —
HOLOFERNES: I also will be naked. (*Pause*)
JUDITH: Yes. Well, that would — that might —
THE SERVANT: This isn't what we expected. Is it? This is far from what —
JUDITH: Be quiet. (*Pause*)
It doesn't help. (*Pause*)
Be quiet. (HOLOFERNES *gets up. The* SERVANT *goes to receive his clothes. He removes them item by item.*)

THE SERVANT (*laying them over her arm*): What lovely stuffs...
HOLOFERNES: Dead men's stuffs.
THE SERVANT: Oh, really?
HOLOFERNES: An army is not honourable, is it?
THE SERVANT: I wouldn't like to say if it is honourable or —
HOLOFERNES: No, it is not honourable, so I make no pretence at honour.
THE SERVANT: I respect that, I really do, and that's a nice piece, too, dead men's, is it? Lovely weave. (*She looks at him.*) You're not that strong, are you? You're not what I'd call powerful. But wiry, are you? Probably you're very fit?
JUDITH: You talk too much.
THE SERVANT: Do I? It's nerves. (*To* HOLOFERNES.) You're stopping there, are you? That's it? (HOLOFERNES *is lightly clad. He does not reply.*) That's it. (*She goes to lay out the clothes.*)
JUDITH: Tomorrow, when you have defeated Israel, as you say you cannot fail to do, how much will you destroy?
HOLOFERNES: All of it.
JUDITH: And the children?
HOLOFERNES: Them I'll enslave.
JUDITH: And the men, you'll —
HOLOFERNES: Cut their throats.
JUDITH: The old men, and the —
HOLOFERNES: If they have throats —
JUDITH: You'll cut them.
HOLOFERNES: Some of this cutting I will do myself.
JUDITH: That's no less than I expected.
HOLOFERNES: I do not distinguish myself from the army. I am cleverer than the army, but not better than the army. I do things they could never do, such as to plot the dispositions. But this does not relieve me of my compact with their vileness. If vileness it is.
JUDITH (*shrugging complacently*): Some would say so.
HOLOFERNES: Some would. I never pay regard to some's opinion. Neither do I laugh at myself. Sometimes, like tonight, I think I want to see a woman naked, but usually, seeing her, I realise it is not what I wanted at all. Generally speaking, I am unhappy until I see the happy, and then I understand the reason for my condition. If I had allowed you to be naked, or you had allowed yourself, I should have dismissed you long before now.
THE SERVANT: Lucky, then! Lucky you —
JUDITH (*hissing*): **You — make — this — so —**
THE SERVANT: Sorry —
JUDITH: **Pitifully — mundane — and —**
THE SERVANT: Sorry —
JUDITH: **Sit — and — watch.** (*The* SERVANT *obeys. A pause.*) I also am unhappy. I believed I was unhappy because I was widowed. But my widowing merely licensed me to show myself for what I am. Everyone else must laugh and smile and greet each other, hoisting

their children in the air and acting the perfect neighbour, whereas I am privileged to wear a melancholy face. Many envy me for this, and men are drawn to unhappy women, as perhaps you know, being subtle. I'm subtle, too. None subtler. She's right, however, you are not well-built. Your power comes from elsewhere, obviously. Am I talking too much? You have revealed so much I feel I should also, but perhaps that's wrong. You might wish me to be silent. You might wish to imagine me rather than to know me. That is the source of desire, in my view. Not what we are, but the possibilities we allow to others to create us. Silence, for example. Might be judged as mystery. (*Long pause. They look at one another.*)

HOLOFERNES: I can't be loved.

JUDITH: So you said.

HOLOFERNES: So if you were thinking of loving me, you would do well to reconsider. (*Pause*)

JUDITH: Yes... (*Pause*) Yes... I came here thinking... what did I think... I —

THE SERVANT: You thought —

JUDITH: **I said to be quiet, didn't I**? (*Pause*)

I came here thinking — obviously — thinking — I love — I — (*Pause*) Never mind, love will do — (*Pause.*) Love the — object — may I call you an object — the object Holofernes — the strategist, the general, the theorist, the murderer, the monster, the hero Holofernes. All those things, which are easy to love. Which are almost a substitute for love. But love is more difficult, it's — **please don't make me go yet**. (*Pause. The* SERVANT *looks anxiously from* JUDITH *to* HOLOFERNES. *The cry of the* SENTRY. *Pause.*)

HOLOFERNES: Let us talk about death.

JUDITH: Yes.

HOLOFERNES: Its ridiculing of life.

JUDITH: Yes.

HOLOFERNES: Its mockery of purpose, its humiliation of —

JUDITH: Yes, yes. (*Pause. He looks at her, while* JUDITH *stares at the ground.*)

HOLOFERNES: We exist for one reason.

JUDITH: One reason? I thought we existed for no reason at all.

HOLOFERNES: To reproduce ourselves. (*Pause. She affects a gasp.*)

JUDITH: That's odd! That — coming from you — is particularly odd because — the pain you've given — and the things you've — to people who have never — and now you say — it is odd. Really, it is odd. I think you have such a beautiful manner. Quite unpredictible.

HOLOFERNES: Given we have no purpose but this eminently absurd purpose it would seem to me it is neither more creditable, nor more dishonourable, to slaughter than to kneel on the cold floor of a monastery. Naturally, I speak from Death's perspective. What other perspective is there?

JUDITH: Yes, but if life is so very — is so utterly — fatuous, should we not comfort one another? Or is that silly? (*Pause*) You think

I'm silly. You're right, I'm only saying this to — I'm spewing the conventional opinion because — when this is such a special night, I really should forbid myself the conventional opinion, even if it is correct, which it may be, even so, however conventional it might be — **and all I wanted was to lie with you.** (*Pause*)

HOLOFERNES: And would that be easier?

JUDITH: Not easier, but. (*Pause*) Not easier at all. (*She draws her garments round her.*)

THE SERVANT: I always said, with love don't ask too many questions. Love's silent, I said. Or it speaks in rather ordinary words. (*She turns to* HOLOFERNES.) Tomorrow you'll be different! You'll have done the killing of a lifetime! Tomorrow you won't know yourself! 'Did I go on about death?' 'Was I miserable?' **Off with yer skirt, darling**! (*She chuckles.*) No, I've seen it. We picked the wrong night. (JUDITH, *with a surge of bravado, gets up.*)

JUDITH: All right, let's fuck.

THE SERVANT: Oh, dear...

JUDITH: I mean, all this — what is all this? You're a general, I'm a widow, so what? You kill thousands, I stay at home, so what? Don't think I haven't met your type before. I have. You want me to plead and pander. I will do. I can do that. You want me to say how much I, how magnificently you, all right, I will do, I'm far from educated, so I'll stop pretending, and anyway, nothing you say is original, either. Do I insult you? Do I abolish your performance? It needs abolishing. (*Pause. The* SERVANT *turns away in despair.* HOLOFERNES *stares at her, without emotion. The pressure in* JUDITH *dissipates. She shrugs.*) I am reckoned to be the most beautiful woman in the district. So I thought I had a chance. (*She goes to pick her clothing off the floor. She stops, and lets out a scream. The scream ceases. She remains still.*)

THE SERVANT: I said to Judith, are you really up to this? Yes, she said. It'll hurt you, I said, one way or another. I know, she said. You'll never be the same, I said. I know that, too, she said. But you can know a thing and still not know it. Now look at us. (*Pause*)

HOLOFERNES: And yet I want to be. (*Pause*) I, the impossible to love, require love. Often, I am made aware of this. (*Pause*)

THE SERVANT: You are? (*Pause*)

HOLOFERNES: This lack.

THE SERVANT: You are, are you?

HOLOFERNES: This lack asserts itself in a distinctive way.

THE SERVANT: Yes?

HOLOFERNES: **Do you think I can't see you**? (*The* SERVANT *is transfixed.*) **Your mask. Your fog. Do you think I can't see you**? (*Pause*) The way in which it asserts itself is as follows. Frequently I expose myself to the greatest danger. I court my own extinction. Whilst I am exhilarated by the conflict I am also possessed of the most perfect lucidity. So absolute am I in consciousness, yet also so removed from fear of death, I am at these moments probably a god. Certainly that is how the enemy perceives me. It is only when the action is over, and I am restored to the weary and sometimes damaged thing that is my body, that I sense a terrible need; not for praise, which I receive in abundance, but of that horror in another that I might have ceased, and had I ceased, she also could not have but ceased. I am not the definition of another's life. That is my absent trophy. I think we live only in the howl of others. The howl is love. (*Pause*)

THE SERVANT: I think, with you, the problem is your strength. Do you mind this? Do you mind if I lecture? I think you probably are perfect. You know too much, which is like armour. Shall I go on? I've seen the hardest whore panic when she could not detect a weakness in the customer. You must give people rights. You must give them their powers over you. Like I step off the pavement for a beggar if he curses me. What has he got? Nothing. Nothing but his curse. So I yield him that. I give him his paltry power. So with you, you must give the woman something to hold over you. You are too perfect. There! End of lecture! (*She turns to* JUDITH.) Are you feeling better, darling? She is not a whore. She is a widow and not a whore. Only with you around, she felt like whoring! (*She laughs. A silence. The cry of the* SENTRY. *Suddenly* HOLOFERNES *clasps the* SERVANT *in his arms, desperately, sobbing quietly. The* SERVANT *looks to* JUDITH. *As suddenly,* HOLOFERNES *releases her.*)

HOLOFERNES: You say I am not weak. I was weak once. None weaker. I crept through life. I staggered from sickness to sickness.

THE SERVANT: I didn't mean that kind of —

HOLOFERNES: I ran from other boys and hid in corners. I sought no company, or the company of girls whose games appeared less brutal, falsely, but. I stammered with shame when asked to speak, even though my mouth was full of language. I lived always in the shadows, hating the sun's glare because it exposed me to the scrutiny of others. **There was none weaker than me.** (*Pause*) But being weak, I discovered cunning. I learned to say one thing, knowing it would satisfy the expectation, whilst carrying on a second and more secret conversation with myself. I led people away from my true intention, my speech became a maze, I used speech to trap my enemies, my speech was a pit, I lived in speech, making it a weapon. And also I learned to run. I practised running, so when speech failed, I could out-distance them. That is how I, the runt, became a general. The mind of the weak-bodied is so terrible, is so out-landish and so subtle. He has made a spiked thing of it, to impale your innocence. (*Pause*)

JUDITH: You mean, nothing you say is true? (*He looks at her.*) I don't mind that. I am perfectly able to lie myself. **I am almost certainly lying now in fact.** (*Pause*)

No, that's —

I'm glad because —

That puts my mind at rest — (*She laughs.*)

Excellent! Because so much is false when men and women are together, so much! I have always thought, when men and women are together, all this is false! And you say — you confess — all is trickery, all is deception, façade and affectation! Excellent! Forgive my hysteria, it was the pressure, the sheer suffocating pressure of sincerity. And now I am light! I am ventilated! A clean, dry wind whirls through my brain! I intend to kill you, how is that for a lie? And that must mean I love you! Or doesn't it? Anything is possible! I think, now we have abandoned the search for truth, really, we can love each other! (*She looks to the* SERVANT.) The relief! (*She laughs again.*) The relief of knowing you are simply an element in a fiction! I think before this moment I never was equipped to love. (*She extends her hand to* HOLOFERNES.) Take my hand! Take my widow's hand in your murderer's hand, my mothering hand in your massacring hand! (*He extends it. She holds it, looks at it.*) It's so white! It's so well cared for. Poets are much grubbier, but they also murder. (*Pause. She kneels beside him.*) Do you like me at all? Of course your reply will be a pack of lies, but. Say anyway. (*Pause*) I spent hours on this get-up. Like a bride. Which is another lie. My lips are not in the least bit red, I am rather pale-mouthed actually. Lies everywhere! Do you like me, though? When you told me you could not help yourself lying I fell in love with you. That was the moment. My husband betrayed me all the time, with girls, but this will be different, won't it? Why girls? Was he ashamed of something? Lie, do lie! (*Pause*)

HOLOFERNES: I know why you're here. (*Pause. The* SERVANT *stares.*)

JUDITH: I know why I came.

HOLOFERNES: I know what you intend.

JUDITH: I know what I intended.

HOLOFERNES: I know it all.

JUDITH: I knew it all. (*Pause*) I knew it all. And now I know nothing. (*He looks into her.*)

HOLOFERNES: We love, then.

JUDITH: Yes.

HOLOFERNES: And I, who is unlovable, I am loved.

JUDITH: My dear, yes... (*Pause*)

THE SERVANT: One of them is lying. Or both of them. This baffles me, because whilst Judith is clever, so is he. Whilst Judith was renowned for being subtle, what else is he? And only six hours to the battle! (*She comes forward.*) The battle begins at dawn. It begins with shouting. They shout for twenty minutes. Yes, a twenty-minute shout! Then they let fly the javelins. Then they shout again. I've seen it. Four times I've seen it. Four times I've run for my life. Our General says we will learn from our mistakes. He says this with a monotonous regularity. We have learned, say the soldiers. We've learned to run the moment we see Holofernes. They look for him. His little form. They see him move his staff — like this — and this — and every movement of his staff brings down an unexpected blow. I run. I jump on the nearest wagon. I whip the horses. Off I go. Fuck the war and fuck the wounded. The whores are miles ahead. The sign of a lost battle is the fleeing whore-carts. Sometimes they pass through towns hours before the army. That's the signal to pack up and go. The whores outrun the cavalry! What strategists they are! What sensibilities! (*To* JUDITH *and* HOLOFERNES.) Shall I leave you, or — (*She sees they are embracing.*) Oh, one of them is lying, but which! (*Pause. She looks from a safe distance, sitting on a pile of clothes.*)

JUDITH: You kiss strangely. I don't criticize, but how strangely you kiss!

HOLOFERNES: And you.

JUDITH: Me?

HOLOFERNES: Your mouth smothers mine, as if it were a hunger. But it might also be — a violence.

JUDITH: And yours is hard. You keep your lips tight-sealed, which might be wonder, or perhaps, are you ashamed? Don't be ashamed. I like your lips.

HOLOFERNES: I can't be loved...!

JUDITH: You are! You are loved!

THE SERVANT: How brilliant she is! How ecstatic she is! She convinces me! But she must be careful, for with lying, sometimes, the idea, though faked, can discover an appeal, and then we're fucked! It's true! I've seen it! I've seen everything!

JUDITH: Shh! (*The* SERVANT *sits again.*) He wants to sleep. (*The* SERVANT *looks puzzled.*) Don't you? You want to sleep...

HOLOFERNES: Yes.

JUDITH: And I know why... (*To the* SERVANT.) **I do know why**! Dear one, you want to sleep because this also has been a battle. Tomorrow we will make love. (*She turns angrily on the* SERVANT.) **It has been a battle for him**!

THE SERVANT: Yes...

JUDITH: A terrible battle for him. To love. To give. (*To the* SERVANT.) And you stare, because he won't make love. You stare, because he does not pull me to the floor. I hate the way you stare! You do hate men! How you hate them!

THE SERVANT: Me?

JUDITH: Yes. For you they have no modesty, their modesty is a sign of impotence. I do hate the way your lip is half-bent in laughter, in contempt, whore!

THE SERVANT (*puzzled*): Who's stopping him sleeping? I'm not!

JUDITH: Whore!

THE SERVANT: Abuse away, dear —

JUDITH: That is real whoring, it is real whoring when a woman mocks the modesty in a man! (*Pause. In the silence, the* SENTRY *cries, and* HOLOFERNES, *wrapped in* JUDITH's *arms, sleeps. A long pause, without movement.*)

THE SERVANT (*abandoning her persona*): Judith...
JUDITH: Shh... (*Pause*) Listen, his breathing, like returning tides...
THE SERVANT: Judith...
JUDITH: Shh... (*Pause*) His moving, like slow cattle on the road...
THE SERVANT: Judith... his sleep is restoring him for slaughter... his strength is the extinction of our race... Judith... his breath is our oblivion... his dreams are our pain... get the sword down, Judith... his luxury is our murder... Judith... his tranquillity is our scream... the sword's up there...
JUDITH: I've seen the sword.
THE SERVANT: Good. Unsheath it.
JUDITH: I hear you. I hear you very clearly.
THE SERVANT: You have a child.
JUDITH: I have a child, yes.
THE SERVANT: Take down the weapon, then.
JUDITH: Yes.
THE SERVANT: Your child sleeps also. Her last sleep if you —
JUDITH: I am not hesitating.
THE SERVANT: You aren't hesitating? What are you doing, then?
JUDITH: I don't know, but you need not urge so. I am not hesitating.
THE SERVANT: You say you are not hesitating, but it looks like hesitation. Take the sword down or I will.
JUDITH: I am absolutely not hesitating.
THE SERVANT: No, but — (*She goes to reach for the sword.*)
JUDITH: **Do not take the sword down.**
THE SERVANT: Israel commands you. Israel which birthed you. Which nourished you. Israel insists. And your child sleeps. Her last sleep if —
JUDITH: **I am well drilled.** (*She glares at the* SERVANT. *The* SENTRY *cries. Pause.* JUDITH *goes to the sword.*)
THE SERVANT: Excellent. (*She unsheaths it.*)
Excellent.
My masterful.
My supreme in.
My most terrible.
My half-divine. (JUDITH *raises the weapon over* HOLOFERNES.)
HOLOFERNES (*without moving*): I'm not asleep. I'm only pretending. (*Pause. The sword stays.*)
My dear.
My loved one.
I'm not asleep. I'm only pretending. (*Pause.* JUDITH *closes her eyes.*)
JUDITH: Why?
THE SERVANT: Don't discuss!
HOLOFERNES: Because I must win everything.
THE SERVANT: Oh, don't discuss! Israel dies if you discuss!
HOLOFERNES: I can win battles. The winning of battles is, if anything, facile to me, but.

JUDITH: My arm aches!
HOLOFERNES: But you.
JUDITH: Aches!
HOLOFERNES: Love.
JUDITH: My arm aches and I lied!
HOLOFERNES: Of course you lied, and I lied also.
JUDITH: We both lied, so —
HOLOFERNES: But in the lies we. Through the lies we. Underneath the lies we.
THE SERVANT: **Oh, the barbaric and inferior vile inhuman bestial and bloodsoaked monster of depravity!**
HOLOFERNES: Judith.
THE SERVANT: **Oh, the barbaric and inferior vile inhuman bestial and bloodsoaked monster of depravity!**
HOLOFERNES: Judith...!
JUDITH: **Oh, the barbaric and inferior** — (*Seeing* JUDITH *is stuck between slogan and action, the* SERVANT *swiftly resorts to a stratagem, and leaning over* HOLOFERNES, *enrages* JUDITH *with a lie.*)
THE SERVANT: He is smiling! He is smiling! (*With a cry*, JUDITH *brings down the sword.*) Goddess! (JUDITH *staggers back, leaving the sword in place. The* SERVANT *leaps to it and saws energetically.*)

Immaculate deliverer!
Oh, excellent young woman!
Oh, virgin!
Oh, widow and mother!
Oh, everything! (*She saws in ecstasy.*)
Fuck this! Hard going, this! (JUDITH *groans, crawling along the floor, and shaking her head from side to side like an animal trapped in a bag. The* SERVANT *ceases her labours. She takes deep breaths.* JUDITH *stops. Long pause.*)
Have you got the bag? (*Pause*)
Judith? (*Pause*)
The bag? (*Pause. She sits, wearily.*)
I do apologize, I thought for — I really do — for one moment, I thought — she won't — she can't — I do apologize — (*Pause*) I will put it in the bag. You needn't. (*Pause*) Ever see it again. (JUDITH *gets up with a strange energy. She dusts off her hands.*)

JUDITH: I was silly there.
THE SERVANT: Oh, I don't know, you —
JUDITH: I was. So fucking silly. Nearly fucked it, didn't I? Nearly fucked it with my. No, I was a silly cunt there, wasn't I?
THE SERVANT: Well, you —
JUDITH: Oh, fuck, yes, a proper slag and bint there —
THE SERVANT: In your pocket I think there's a —
JUDITH: A right bitch cunt, I was, nearly bollocked it, eh, nearly

— (*She staggers.*) **Oh, my darling how I** — (*She recovers.*) Nearly poxed the job, the silly fucker I can be sometimes, a daft bitch and a cunt brained fuck arse — (*She staggers.*) **Oh, my — Oh, my —**

THE SERVANT: The bag. Give me the bag.

JUDITH: **Oh, my — Oh, my —**

THE SERVANT: **Give it to me, then.** (*Pause.* JUDITH *stabilizes herself.*) We take the head because the head rewards the people. The people are entitled symbolically to show contempt for their oppressor. Obviously the spectacle has barbaric undertones but we. The concentration of emotion in the single object we etcetera. So. (JUDITH *is still.*) All right, I'll wrap it in a sheet. (*She pulls a cloth from the wall and begins with a will to wrap the severed head.*)

JUDITH: I want to fuck. (*Pause. The* SERVANT *stops.*)

THE SERVANT: Lie down. Rest for a little while, then we can —

JUDITH: No, I must fuck. I must. (*Pause*)

THE SERVANT: With who do you —

JUDITH: With him. I want to fuck with him. (*Pause*)

THE SERVANT: You are in such a state, my dear, and I do understand, but —

JUDITH: I can arouse him. He is still warm, so obviously I can arouse him. (*She moves towards the body.*)

THE SERVANT: Sit down, and count to a hundred —

JUDITH: You count to a hundred, I'll arouse him, look! (*She draws back the cloths, exposing him to herself.*) Oh, look... !

THE SERVANT: **Get away from him.**

JUDITH (*touching him with innocence*): It curls... it moves like weed in the slow current of my gaze...

THE SERVANT: **Vile and dishonourable** —

JUDITH: Shh! Shh! Do look, the strange and mobile nature of him here, a landscape, look, I never saw my husband so revealed, so innocent and simple, I must arouse him.

THE SERVANT (*attempting coolness*): Don't do that with an enemy —

JUDITH: An enemy?

THE SERVANT: It demeans your triumph and humiliates our —

JUDITH: How can he be an enemy? His head is off.

THE SERVANT: **Enemy. Vile enemy.**

JUDITH: You keep saying that... ! But now the head is gone I can make him mine, surely? The evil's gone, the evil's in the bag and I can love! Look, I claim him! Lover, lover, respond to my adoring glance, it's not too late, is it? We could have a child, we could, come, come, adored one, it is only politics kept us apart!

THE SERVANT: I think I am going to be sick...

JUDITH: No, no, count to a hundred...

THE SERVANT: I will be made insane by this!

JUDITH: You weren't insane before. Is it love makes you insane? Hatred you deal admirably with. Come, loved one... ! (*She lies over* HOLOFERNES's *body. The* SERVANT *is transfixed with horror.*)

He doesn't move...

He doesn't move... ! (*Slowly, reluctantly, she climbs off the body. She sits among the wreckage of the bed. The cry of the* SENTRY. *A long pause. The* SERVANT *looks at* JUDITH.)

THE SERVANT: Judith...

JUDITH: Yes...

THE SERVANT: I think we must —

JUDITH: Yes —

THE SERVANT: Or it'll be —

JUDITH: It will be, yes —

THE SERVANT: Dawn and —

JUDITH: Exactly. (*Pause.* JUDITH *doesn't move. The* SERVANT *kneels beside her.*)

THE SERVANT: I will find you a husband. Such a fine man and he will make you laugh but also fill you with admiration. He will have both wit and intelligence. And the wit will not demean him, nor the intelligence make him remote.

JUDITH: Difficult...

THE SERVANT: Difficult, yes, but I will find him. And he will give you children. He will be a child with them and a man with you. And his childishness will never mock his manliness, nor his manliness oppress the child.

JUDITH: Difficult...

THE SERVANT: Difficult, yes, but I will discover him. And old women will smile at your radiant delight, and silences will fall between you born of perfect understanding, so deep will be your mutuality speech will be redundant, such a bond, oh, such a union, the plants will thrive on your allotments from your tender touch, get up now. (*Pause*)

JUDITH: I can't. (*Pause*)

THE SERVANT: You can't... ?

JUDITH: Move. (*Pause. She stares at the* SERVANT *in horror.*)

THE SERVANT: Judith —

JUDITH: **Can't move**! (*Pause. The* SERVANT *subdues her irritation.*)

THE SERVANT: What are you saying? I'm full of patience but. All sympathy and tolerance but. A hard night this, admittedly but. **If they catch us it's wombs to the Alsatians, bitch**! (*Pause*)

JUDITH: Listen —

THE SERVANT: All right —

JUDITH: Are you listening —

THE SERVANT: Yes —

JUDITH: Because I have no more wish to be —

THE SERVANT: All right —

JUDITH: Than you have —

THE SERVANT: All right, all right —

JUDITH: I am fixed to the ground, do you follow me, I am unable to move, I have the will but not the power —

THE SERVANT: Yes —

JUDITH: I'm stuck, **I'm stuck**. (*Pause. The* SERVANT *looks around, anxiously, then with resolution, goes to lift* JUDITH. JUDITH *lets out a cry of pain.*)
JUDITH: It hurts!
THE SERVANT: What, what hurts?
JUDITH: Don't touch me, please!
THE SERVANT: Don't touch you?
JUDITH: Please, don't touch me again... ! (*Pause. The* SERVANT *wipes her palms on her skirt, nervously. She walks swiftly up and down, stops.*)
THE SERVANT: God's punished you. (*Pause*)
JUDITH: What.
THE SERVANT: God has.
JUDITH: Why.
THE SERVANT: Obviously.
JUDITH: Why.
THE SERVANT: For —
JUDITH: What!
THE SERVANT: Just now. With him.
JUDITH: Punished me?
THE SERVANT: You have offended Him! (*Pause*) I can't come near you, in case — can't possibly — in case — He might — (JUDITH *emits a long wail.*) Obviously, you're judged and — (*The wail rises.*) Plead! Plead with Him! (*She stares at* JUDITH. *Pause.*) All right, I will. (*She kneels.*) And if it fails, I have to go, forgive me, but —
JUDITH: No, don't do that, I —
THE SERVANT: **Have to obviously**. (*She stares at* JUDITH.)
Take the head and. (*Pause*)
Obviously. (*Pause*)
You will be honoured. All Israel will. And streets will be. And parks. Great thoroughfares. Whatever you suggest. (*Pause*)
JUDITH: Plead! (*The* SERVANT *concentrates.*) Louder!
THE SERVANT: I am, but —
JUDITH: Louder, then! (*The* SERVANT *rocks to and fro on her knees, then stops. She scrambles to her feet.*)
THE SERVANT: I think you must do it.
JUDITH: He wants me to die!
THE SERVANT: I don't think we can make assumptions of that sort but — (*She finds the head, and wraps it swiftly.*)
JUDITH: Yes! Hates me and wants me to die!
THE SERVANT: I'm sorry but — (JUDITH *lets out a profound cry of despair as the* SERVANT, *clasping the head, goes to the door. She stops. She looks back at* JUDITH. *Pause.*) I say God. I mean Judith. (*Pause*) I say Him. But I mean you. (*Pause. The cry of the* SENTRY *is heard. The* SERVANT *places the head on the ground, and comes back to* JUDITH. *She kneels before her, and leaning on*

her knuckles, puts her forehead to the ground. Pause. JUDITH *watches.*)

JUDITH: You are worshipping me.
Aren't you? Worshipping me?
Why are you doing that?

THE SERVANT: Not for what you are.

JUDITH: No?

THE SERVANT: For what you will be.

JUDITH: When?

THE SERVANT: When you stand, Judith.

JUDITH: I can't stand... (*Pause*)

THE SERVANT: Firstly, remember we create ourselves. We do not come made. If we came made, how facile life would be, worm-like, crustacean, invertebrate. Facile and futile. Neither love nor murder would be possible. Secondly, whilst shame was given us to balance will, shame is not a wall. It is not a wall, Judith, but a sheet rather, threadbare and stained. It only appears a wall to those who won't come near it. Come near it and you see how thin it is, you could part it with your fingers. Thirdly, it is a facility of the common human, but a talent in the specially human, to recognise no act is reprehensible but only the circumstances make it so, for the reprehensible attaches to the unnecessary, but with the necessary, the same act bears the nature of obligation, honour, and esteem. These are the mysteries which govern the weak, but in the strong, are staircases to the stars. I kneel to you. I kneel to the Judith who parts the threadbare fabric with her will. Get up, now. (*Pause.* JUDITH *cannot move. The* SERVANT *counts the seconds. She perseveres.*) Judith, who are those we worship? What is it they possess? The ones we wrap in glass and queue half-fainting for a glimpse? The ones whose works are quoted and endorsed? The little red books and the little green books, Judith, who are they? Never the kind, for the kind are terrorized by grief. Get up now, Judith. (*Nothing happens. Pause*) No, they are the specially human who drained the act of meaning and filled it again from sources fresher and — (JUDITH *climbs swiftly to her feet.*)

JUDITH: You carry the head until we reach the river. Then I'll carry it. (*She busily goes to the sword.*) The sword I'm taking with us. (*The* SERVANT, *amazed and gratified, starts to scramble to her feet.*) **Who said you could get up**. (*Pause. The* SERVANT *smiles, weakly.*) Beyond the river, you walk behind me. Ten yards at least.

THE SERVANT: Yes. Good. (*She starts to rise again.*)

JUDITH: **Who said you could get up**. (*The* SERVANT *stops.*) And any version that I tell, endorse it. For that'll be the truth.

THE SERVANT: Absolutely — (*She moves again.*)

JUDITH: **Who said you could get up**. (*The* SERVANT *freezes, affecting amusement.*)

THE SERVANT: I was only thinking —

JUDITH: Thinking? I do that.

THE SERVANT: Wonderful!
JUDITH: In fact, looking at you as I do, I find your posture contains so many elements of mute impertinence.
THE SERVANT: Honestly?
JUDITH: Honestly, yes. Your head, for example, presumes the vertical.
THE SERVANT: I'll stoop. (*She lowers her head. Pause.* JUDITH *comes close, kneeling beside her.*)
JUDITH: I shall so luxuriate in all the honours, I do not care what trash they drape me with, what emblems or what diadems, how shallow, glib and tinsel all the medals are, **I'll sport them all** — (*The* SERVANT *goes as if to embrace her.*) **Don't shift you intellectual bitch**! (*The* SERVANT *stoops again, laughing with delight.*) No, I shall be unbearable, intolerably vile, inflicting my opinions on the young, I shall be the bane of Israel, spouting, spewing, a nine-foot tongue of ignorance will slobber out my mouth and drench the populace with the saliva of my prejudice, they will wade through my opinions, they will wring my accents out their clothes, but they will tolerate it, for am I not their mother? Without me none of them could be born, **He said so**. (*Pause*)
THE SERVANT: Yes. To everything. Shall I get up?
JUDITH: No, filth.
THE SERVANT: I was only thinking —
JUDITH: Thinking? I do that.
THE SERVANT (*with a short laugh*): Yes! I forgot! But it occurs to me, time is —
JUDITH: No hurry, filth. Sit still. (*Pause. The* SERVANT *stares at the ground.* JUDITH *walks round her, holding the sword.*) Filth —
THE SERVANT: Do you have to call me —
JUDITH: Filth, put your teeth against my shoe. (*A black pause.*) Filth, do. (*The* SERVANT *inclines her head to* JUDITH's *foot, and is still.*) I think I could cut off a million heads and go home amiable as if I had been scything in the meadow. Clean this. (*She holds out the weapon. The* SERVANT *goes to wipe the blade on a cloth.*) No, silly, with your hair. (*Pause*)
THE SERVANT: Now, listen —
JUDITH: **You listen**. (*The* SERVANT *anxiously regards the door. She takes the weapon and cleans it with her hair. She lays the weapon down, goes to stand.* JUDITH's *foot constrains her. Pause.*) Your hair's vile.
THE SERVANT: Obviously, I have just —
JUDITH: Cut it off, then. (*With a weary movement, the* SERVANT, *affecting patience, leans forward on her hands.*)
THE SERVANT: Judith...
JUDITH: **Must! Must!** (*Pause. The* SERVANT *lifts the weapon again.*) To kill your enemies, how easy that is. To murder the offending, how oddly stale. Real ecstasy must come of liquidating innocence, to punish in the absence of offence **You haven't done it yet** that

must be the godlike act, when there is perfect incomprehension in the victim's eyes I will if you won't! (*The* SERVANT, *in an ecstasy of disgust, hacks her hair. She is still again.*) Later, we'll crop it. What you've done is such a mess.

THE SERVANT: Yes...

JUDITH: Well, isn't it?

THE SERVANT: Whatever you say.

JUDITH: Whatever I say, yes. (*Pause.* JUDITH *walks over the stage, looking at the still form of the* SERVANT. *She walks back again, stops.*)

I'm trying to pity you.
But it's difficult because.
Because for you nothing is really pain at all.
Not torture. Death. Or.
Nothing is.
It's drained, and mulched, and used to nourish further hate, as dead men's skulls are ground for feeding fields...

THE SERVANT: Whatever you say.

JUDITH: Whatever I say, yes.

THE SERVANT (*seeing the slow spread of light*): There's light under the flaps. It's dawn, Judith.

JUDITH: Dawn! Yes! This is the hour sin slips out the sheets to creep down pissy alleys! Morning, cats! Did you slither, also? Morning, sparrows! Rough night? Hot beds cooling. The running of water. Well, it has to end at some time, love! But its smell, in the after hours... Magnificence! (*She laughs, with a shudder. A cracked bell is beaten monotonously.*)

Israel!
Israel!
My body is so
Israel!
My body has no
Israel!
Israel!
My body was but is no longer
Israel
Is
My
Body!

The cracked bell stops. Sounds of naturalistic conversation, the clatter of pots, the rising of a camp. The SERVANT *gets up. She goes to* JUDITH *and kisses her hands. Taking the head in the bag, she slips out of the tent.* JUDITH *does not follow at once.*